# Ruminating Years

Written by:
Artem Vaskanyan

Cadmus Publishing
www.cadmuspublishing.com

# A Short Biography of Artem Vaskanyan

Ever since I was a kid, I wanted to write, but I could never attend school like a normal kid. Since my family always moved around like some gypsies in a caravan, it became impossible for me to learn and pursue my dream.

I was born in Baku, Azerbaijan, a place that is well known for black caviar and rich oil fields. At age seven my family and I had to flee the country for our lives when the war between Armenia and Azerbaijan broke out over disputed land. Since we were Armenians and Christians staying in a Muslim country was not safe. Before I could finish first grade, I was on a train traveling north to the Russian parts of the Soviet Union; where we continued to move from one province, town, and city to another every few months, preventing me to stay in school.

Eventually, my family and I came to the United States in 1993, when I was only thirteen and with a second-grade education. For the first seven years that I lived in the U.S. my lifestyle was not any different. As a matter of fact, it became even more difficult due to the lack of speaking the language, affecting a way to earn money and struggling to acclimatize. All of this contributed to my incarceration where I began to pursue my education, first on my own, and then over a decade later enrolling in a prison education program that offered B.L.S. Interdisciplinary Studies by Boston University. For the past six and a half years I have attended BU and have successfully graduated in 2020.

Nowadays I write short (fictional) stories and surprisingly have found a passion to write poems, which I would love to share with you all.

Enjoy!


Sincerely,

ARTEM VASKANYAN

# To Readers

As an immigrant and a refugee, migrating from country to countries and from place to place since my childhood, up until being arrested and then incarcerated, made me look at life not through my eyes but through my heart. My life experience had taught me how to pay attention more to the persons' internal side, rather than external; since this is where the true essence of a person lies. 'Ruminating Years' is about love and despair, happiness and loss, humor, sarcasm, and spiritual and intellectual growth. It consists of seventy-four epic and short poems through which I reveal my life's epic journey while living in the Soviet Union and then in the United States, and where I've endured great suffering and loss. In the process I was able to transform my failures, mistakes, and misfortunes into at least some achievements during my incarceration.

'Ruminating Years' has taken years to complete as it was revised and shared with my friends and other poets and English professors at Boston University prison program.

Please keep in mind that some of my poetry can be offensive. If I managed to create with some of my poems an empowering, or a pleasant feeling and, or stir emotions of disgust and anger then I've fulfilled my purpose as a poet.

In order to create empowering poems that could move my readers, I had to put aside my personal opinions of what other people might think of me. I needed to make a sacrifice to get my point across. If I were to care about other's feelings while creating poetry then all of my poems would have been subjective, and I would be a fraud and a fool to try to please everyone.

Poetry is an art,
And an art has no place
For cowards, frauds and fools.

Kindly,
ARTEM VASKANYAN

# For My Grandparents

Who gave me warmth and light
In cold and dark places
With their kind words.

# FOR ALL

Who ran out of time,
Before they could unshackle themselves
From their soul-crushing mindset.

# Ruminating Years
# By Artem Vaskanyan
In Chronological Order:

# You

By Artem Vaskanyan

I never knew what love was like,
Nor being happy felt.
There was no joy, no laughter,
Only sadness in my heart,
Surrounded by unloved
Who showed me no compassion
Or what it was to feel alive.

I felt alone and full of sadness at all times,
My heart consumed by darkness,
And loss of breath and light.

There were no hugs, no kisses,
Only a cold touch descended upon my heart.
No mother's love to caress me,
Nor father who never had a chance
To show his love.
And those who tried were taken
By the one who sees it all.

I only knew of sadness, hate, despair,
The bitterness of life and death too well.
Of love, but only in a distant dream,
Until I met you.

In time, my heart began to melt,
And I could feel the warmth of love
Flowing in my veins.

Your love had melted all the grief,
And everything else that darkness had created.

When you come closer,
My heart beats faster with every step you take.
Because of you,
I think of love more than I ever dreamed.

Until I met you,
There was no light in the sky
To guide me through my life,
No warmth to give me strength,
No love to feel alive,
And no future to think about;
Life had no purpose,
Life was death,
Until you found me, and I, you.

You are my life,
My light,
My joy,
My love,
My only family.

But, when I said these words to you,
You smiled lovingly at me,
Lying next to me in bed.
I stroke your hair
Gently with my hand,

You vanished into thin air,
Like a cloud dissipates from a light breeze.
A distant dream that's all it was,
But, you were, much more than that to me.

-2017

# TINY ROOMS

By Artem Vaskanyan

I spent most of my life
Living in tiny rooms
Not knowing what freedom was
Or how it felt to be alive.
And when I wasn't in prison yet
I was confined to work,
To money, to the bills,
That I was enslaved to.
Not by choice, but by an obligation to survive.
Is freedom in part being in caged,
And being part of an illusion?
I often think behind my own private walls.
My soul cries for freedom
That I never had a taste to enjoy.
What is freedom?
Again, I ask myself,
Yet can't find an answer
To my relentless question.
I know what freedom isn't!
But what it is;
I still haven't had a chance
To have a taste to enjoy.
How can I say
That I know what freedom is
When till this day
I still live in tiny rooms.

- 2018

# THE FORGOTTEN ONE
By Artem Vaskanyan

I am whose roots had been forgotten,
But not entirely lost.

I am a great grandson
Of a genocide survivor,
Whom Ottoman butchers did not get
With their atrocities.

I am who knows all too well
What it means to be forgotten,
And lost in a foreign land.

October, 2018

# THIRTY-NINE

By Artem Vaskanyan

Today I'm thirty-nine!
And I feel like an old man
Who is ninety-nine,
Not in body but in mind.

My body aches from time to time,
While my mind is in distress
Most of the time.
It is exhausted not from work
Or exercise,
But from restless thoughts
That drive me crazy
In the middle of the night.

It thinks of years
That had been lost
And can never be forgotten
Or revived.

I hate that number thirty-nine!
And any number that has a nine.
It makes me feel
As though I'm about to face the end.
The end of life that I
Haven't scratched the surface
As of yet.

Today I'm thirty-nine!
And, Yes!
I have lived
A long unpleasant life.

From choices made by me,
But mostly by those
Who were too close to me.

How many birthdays are there left
For me to celebrate?
Before it would be my last,
To bury me at last,
No. Wait!
Just to make sure,
If I do drop dead for sure,
Then I would rather be cremated,
Than be a food for worms
Behind sealed coffin doors.

And don't forget to scatter
What's left of me
From the high above
Preferably from the mountain
Of Ararat.

Today I'm thirty-nine!
And, I like to think that I
Sculpt my own life
With both my bare hands.

And, even though, so many of my plans
Are left unfinished and undone
From living in a place
Where people perish every day,
But here I am,
For some unknown reason
Continue to persevere and plan ahead
For a life that I might never even get.

Perhaps, it is not in my nature
To fall apart.
Or maybe I'm just too stubborn
To accept the life
That I so desperately despise.

For a man as I,
Who is driven to survive
And persevere in this savage life,
Not by choice,
But from some unknown desire
To overcome this soul-depriving life;

To fall apart
Would be a sin
Against all mankind
Who is trying to survive.

It is true!
I'm my own worst enemy at times.
I see this clearly now.
Why can't I just
Sit, shut up,
And wait for things to come?
Like many other men do around me
All the time.

Why do I
Have to fight and struggle
To live my life?
I ask myself this question quite often
When I'm alone,
And I'm alone the entire time.

As far as I'm concerned
This could be my last year
To celebrate.
So, I have no other choice,
But to plan
And do what I possibly can
In this life,
Before it all comes to an end.

Today I'm thirty-nine!
I feel exhausted
Not from age
But from a life
That just won't change.

November, 2019

# The Wooden Box
### By Artem Vaskanyan

I never had a chance to bury her
Or to even say goodbye.

Her ashes were placed inside the wooden box
Where it still remains
Somewhere in my mother's house till this day.

They say, "it is waiting for your return.
For you and only you along to bury her
As she would've wanted all along."

Before she died, she lost her mind
From not wanting to accept the fact
That I won't come back to her on time.

She couldn't face the fact
That I will spend most of my life
Behind the prison walls.

At least her soul is finally at rest
From a long turmoil
Of my absence in her life.

I used to tell her
While holding my tears back.
Don't worry!
I'm fine! I'm fine!
Everything will be Okay!

I told her that for sixteen long years,
Not realizing myself

That this was all only a beginning.

She passed away without me knowing,
But when I fall asleep,
I can hear her voice calling.

And, even though she's gone,
The vivid memories of her remain.
Reminding me of love
And that there is still some hope
To have a better life someday.

She took the place of my own mother
Who never cared for me,
Or my older brother.

And she even managed to replace
My poor father,
Who died months before my birth.

We trusted and loved each other dearly,
Like mother and son should've always had.

Our unconditional love for each other
Has always been there for one another.
But the trust was something different.
It developed over time
In a place of misery and despair,

Where we both realized,
Since the early beginning
That it can only tear us apart,
Or bring us closer to a new beginning.

Lucky me,
I had her love and trust
That I would've never got
From any living person on this earth.

Yet, I'm not sure I can say the same
About my father,
Since I heard he loved my grandmother.

January 19, 2019

# THE RAINSTORM, COMING!

By Artem Vaskanyan

I walked through the alley
Between tall trees and Lilac bushes
And stumbled upon the meadow,
It was covered with various types
Of mushrooms from Shitake to Morels.

Further ahead behind the Blueberry bushes
A crystal clear pond emerged.
It welcomed any living being to take a swim.

The leaves of many trees surrounding the pond
Worked like umbrellas,
Catching every rain drop
That descended from above.

The rain dropped from the clouds
Upon the surface of the still water,
Creating micro explosions with each drop.

A murder of crows flew across the sky
And disappeared into dark clouds.

The sun was long gone,
Consumed by the giant cloud
That turned the light to darkness
In the blink of an eye.

The lightning flashed before my eyes,
My heart skipped beats,
And my bones felt chill
As cold wind picked up

And swayed the trees from side to side.

The leaves begun to rustle
Whispering into my ears,
Of the danger,
That the rainstorm, coming!

January, 2019

# BEFORE I GO AWAY

By Artem Vaskanyan

One bullet in a chamber.
An index finger on a trigger.
Barrel pointed to my head.
At any moment to discharge
And take away
What's left of life.

Another day had passed.
Another life went to waste.
A reminder to myself
That I,
Could be the next.

Could this be my day
To finally depart?
I think from time to time.
But no one knows for sure,
Besides the one
Who holds a barrel to my head.

It could be this day
Or the next,
When the trigger is pulled,
And my life
Would become a waste.

And when it does.
My only wish to say,
A quick prayer
Before I go away.

January, 2019

# Washed Up Gangsters
By Artem Vaskanyan

I see old washed up gangsters
Around me all the time.
An old gangster in particular
Who did his time-
Too many times before
And here he is
Came back again for more.

From what I knew,
He didn't roll on his crew,
Instead he took a hit
For all whom he knew.
And just like that
He went to prison
This time for life.

From what I saw,
When he came back in
He was as tough as nails.
And many cons
Loved and payed respect to him
For what he stood.

For his code of silence
And for his way of life,
It gave him stripes,
The same stripes that he so proudly
Displayed around cons.

Unfortunately, they judged him
For the way he used to be,

And disregarded to see
For the man he became to be.

From what I heard,
This old G[1]
Might've been a solid,
Tough, deadly Mafioso
A lifetime ago.

But, nowadays he is not even
Half a man he used to be.
Instead, this old washed up gangster
Has lost his way,
And ratting on fellow cons
Became one of his favored way.

And there are many more like him.
The same old washed up gangsters
Who dry snitch on cons
Behind closed doors
Every time they get a chance.

Another old G
That comes to mind.
Who till this day will gladly fight
And even die for his beliefs.

He won't rat,
Or run from a bloody fight,
But he will gladly chase you men
Who ended up in prison at a young age.

Who knew that this old man will break down and become a queer.

1        Gangster.

The same exact queer
Who he gay bashed
In front of his fellow cons
For nothing more than just for laughs.

But, nowadays his only goal in life
Is to be a good chicken hawk[2]
Who chases cock.

It's true!
What some cons say,
That rats aren't born
They are made.
And that chicken hawks
Love to manipulate.

Especially those young men
Who revere them
For what they think they are.

It's funny from where I stand
To see how blind people are.
Who love old washed up gangsters
For what they think they are, -
Nothing more than a façade.

I'm not saying that all old G's
Are that –
Only that
Many are exactly
What I said they are.

February, 2019
_____
2       An old man seeks young men to have sex with.

# Poison Ivy

By Artem Vaskanyan

Her favored flower
Is a poison Ivy.
Her favored color, red.
The color of the blood
As she once said.
No wonder I regret
The first time when we met.

Her love is like poison Ivy
That spreads along my skin
Infecting every inch
Of my mind and body.
The itch is irresistible
Just as her love.
The more you scratch
The more it itches
And the more you fall in love.
No wonder people always said,
To get as far away from her
While there is still a chance.
She broke my heart
Too many times before,
And still I don't learn,
I go back to her for more.
No wonder she likes vodka
Without ice,
She is cold as ice.

She has no beating heart.
Her heart doesn't sound
Like a beating drum.

Instead, it sounds
Like a thunder in the sky.
No wonder dark clouds burst
Over her every time.

She is an evergreen,
Who never stops to be
At what she is.
Her poison doesn't disappear,
But only grows stronger
With every season as she spreads.
No wonder flowers drop dead
Around her where they stand.

As poisonous as she is.
The feel of pleasure and the pain
Is a perfect blend
To make me feel alive.
No wonder I don't care
When people call me,
A sucker for love.

The soul attracts
What it desires,
And what I desire
Is a woman like her.
Who never stops to be
At what she is,
And what she does
To those who fall in love with her.
No wonder I can't bear
To live another day without her.

I know you can tell a lot

About a woman who says,
Her favored flower is a poison Ivy.
But you have no idea!
How beautiful she looks
In a red dress
Surrounded by the poison Ivy,
And an Ivy flower inserted
In her long black hair.

March, 2019

# THE WHEEL BARROW
By The Name Lucy
By Artem Vaskanyan

One wheel in the front,
Two handles in the rear,
And a shape of a barrel
In the center.

She comes in my favorite color, Red.
She is my favorite gadget
Who saves me time
To do my arduous work on the farm.

Besides providing for the White Chickens,
She carries farm tools to the fields.
Along with heavy stones
To repair dilapidated walls.
Bags of grain to feed
The chickens and the ducks,
Hay for cows
And the rest of the four legged animals
Who live with me on a farm.

She helps me carry
The heavy loads of fruits and vegetables
To sell at the Farmer's Market.
Where I walk with her for miles
On every weekend morning,
And bring back groceries
To feed my family.

The Wheel Barrow,
Is like my second wife,

I never had.
She saves me time
But most importantly my health.

She is more helpful
Than my nagging wife
Who does her part of work
Inside the house,
But when it comes to work outside
In rain and snow
She is nowhere to be found.

I depend on my second wife
To survive.
That is why is spend
Most of my time with her,
Rather than with my wife.

My wife gets jealous,
When I call her Lucy.
She says,
I have lost my mind!

But I say to her
Woman!
You don't know!
What it does to a man
Alone on the field
With no one to help him with his work
But a Wheel Barrow
By the name Lucy.

ᶜarch, 2019

# My First Tooth
By Artem Vaskanyan

My mother took me to the dentist
Instead of the Toy store as she promised.
I wish I would've never told her
Of the tooth ache that I had.
That morning she said,
"Let's go buy you a toy
That will take your tooth ache away."
Elated I became,
Got dressed and even forgot about the pain.
Only five years young at that time,
My instinct told me for the first time
In my life,
That something didn't smell right.
We walked in the opposite direction
Of the Toy store
At an extremely unusual fast pace,
Like we were late for something important.
The office building was just like
Any other building in the city.
But inside, people were all dressed in white,
Like ghosts.
There was a long hallway
Full of doors on both sides.
The waiting room was filled with kids
Like me,
All tricked by mothers as tall
As mine.
Kids sitting,
Clutching to their treacherous,
Cunning mothers
With an expectation to be next

In line to buy a toy.
But when one of our comrades came out
Of the room with tears in his eyes.
Crying,
Holding the side of his cheek
With both hands
And with every step
He took,
He looked up at his mom
In disbelief.
Saying with his big eyes in a language
That any kid can understand,
"Bitch, what the Hell!
How could you do this to me!
Me!
Your own son!"
Dead silence broke
Among the young and old.
The secret was out,
There was no toy.
The only part that was unknown,
Who will be next in line
To buy a toy.
There was nothing that could've been done.
We couldn't possibly get up and run.
Our short legs were no match
For our long legged mothers
On high heels.
Despite the fact
That I was the fastest kid
In the back yard.
There simply wasn't enough room
To sprint,
And even then

I couldn't possibly break free
From my mom's gorilla grip.
There was no escape.
My fate was destined,
My fate was sealed
In this scary place.
I accepted it,
And hoped for the best.
I even prayed in silence
For this moment to end.
It wasn't the fate that drove me nuts,
But the waiting in line
Was more like waiting
For my turn to go to Hell.
It wasn't long
Until I heard my name called
By the skinny blond nurse
Who looked more like a toothpick
Than a real nurse.
Usually when someone calls my name,
I jump up with excitement
To hear what they have to say.
But not today.
I've been tricked too many times
In one damn day.
I kept silent,
As my mom continued
To gossip with her friend.
I quietly whispered to the nurse,
"He is not here!
He must've left!"
But wait!
My mother overheard her call again,
And dry snitched me

To the skinny ass nurse.
She got up,
Still holding my hand
Lifting me from my stool
As we went.
We entered the dentist office
And I was seated on the metal chair
That was as cold as ice,
Right next to the wooden table
That looked exactly like a table
In my kitchen room.
And there on that big round table
In order displayed
All the dentist's shiny tools
From small to larger
And even larger.
I thought for a second
Were these the toys for me to choose?
The dentist entered,
And said,
"Hello!"
She was as big as the closet
In my dining room.
At first I didn't notice
How huge her hands were
Not until, she said,
"Open wide!"
And stuck her hand
Into my mouth,
Followed by the pliers
In her other hand.
These were the same kind of pliers
That I often saw my Grandfather
Working with around the house.

These pliers that I admired
Not too long ago
Were now inserted into my mouth
Gripping tightly to my aching tooth.
I squinted my eyes
And cried like hell
And called them both
By many names
With my mouth wide open.
My mother held my hands
Down to the chair,
As I tried to fight them off.
The nurse with the large hands,
Yelled.
"Hold him steady!
Hold him still!"
While pulling and wiggling
Back and forth,
From side to side
My tooth with pliers.
She pulled it out
With all her might!
Smiling and proud.
If there was Hell!
This must be it.
The pain I felt
Was more than anything
I ever felt throughout my life,
I don't remember the dentist's face,
But I do remember blacking out
And seeing stars.
You must be thinking,
What the hell!
How come my mom

Didn't ask for Anesthetic?
To tell the truth.
Back in '85
In one of the republics
Of the Soviet Union.
This kind of stuff wasn't available.
Not even for the kids my age.
This is not America!
And I don't expect you
To understand.
Nor do I want your sympathy
Or any kind of empathy.
But this must explain
If you ever wondered why
People from U.S.S.R.
Are scared to see the dentist
Till this day.
I left the office
Holding with a hand
My swollen cheek,
And with the other
I held my tooth in the open hand.
I cried,
Just like any other
That came before me.
I even gave
My mom the look.
But I never felt more proud
And even happier
From getting,
My first tooth pulled.

March, 2019

# THOSE WHOSE ARE LOCKED UP
By Artem Vaskanyan

If you are one of those who are locked up,
Then you have to be careful!
Not to have too much fun in prison,
Or you might just forget
The beauty of freedom.

If you continue to over-indulge yourself with:
Playing games,
Watching the Idiot-Box,
Getting high on K-2 and drunk of homebrew,
Chilling with the crew,
Gambling away every last $
That you mom sends to you,
(So you could eat a little better
Than that state-crap you find
Three times a day
On your plastic tray)

Then, how do you expect to become refined,
And understand the reason why
You ended up confined.
When all that you are concerned with
Is to escape the reality of prison life.

The prison is to make you realize
What you have lost,
What you are missing,
And not to replace your life
With the one without freedom.

The prison is not where you belong.

It is no place for any human with a soul.
Regardless, what other people say
About those who made mistakes,
Who took their life for granted,
And ended up to be condemned
To live a life without freedom.

May, 2019

# IT'S AMAZING
By Artem Vaskanyan

It's Amazing how not too long ago
You've been at the bottom of the Cesspool:
Looked upon like some kind of Object,
Talked to like a Child,
Spat out like some Spit,
Walked upon like some dirty Carpet,
Scrapped off of a frying Pan
Like charred Food, like some Gum
Stuck to the bottom of the Shoe,
Shattered to pieces like a glass Vase,
Kicked around like a stray Dog,
Stripped to nakedness like a Whore,
Deprived of manhood like a castrated Bull,
Kept in a cage longer than any Animal,
Flushed down the toilet like an Excrement,
Disassembled like an old useless Car,
Discarded like a cut out Cancer,
Pronounced dead without being checked
For any signs of Life,
Buried alive like some Corpse.
It's amazing, how after all of this
You're still here, Alive and Well.

May, 2019

# WHEN I TOLD THEM . . .

By Artem Vaskanyan

When I told them that I wore Galoshes[3]
Throughout most of my childhood years,
Instead of Jordans.
Not only did they laugh at me,
But they made me feel like I was worthless
Who did not deserve to wear a pair of Jordans.

When I told them that I had eggs
For breakfast, lunch and dinner
Throughout most of my life.
Not only did they laugh at me,
But they also teased me with a burger
And called me 'Eggs" like it was my name.

When I told them that I went to school,
But, only up to the second grade,
And that by the age of twenty-nine
Was when I read my first book,
Not only did they laugh at me,
But they also called me 'Moron'
Who should go back to school
To repeat the second grade again.

When I told them that my mother
Never cared about me,
And that my stepfather
Always beat the heck out of me,
Not only did they laugh at me,
But they also said,
We don't blame your mother

---

3       Galoshes – rubber shoes worn in wet weather.

For not giving a damn about you
Or your stepfather for beating the heck out of you.

And when I told them that I've been in prison,
Since I was twenty years old,
Not only did the laugh even harder at me,
But they also said,
This is where I belonged to be.

But, when I told them that I've graduated from (B.U.)[4]
With B.L.S., In Liberal Arts,
Speak fluently three languages and some,
Forgave my mother, stepfather
And all the rest who caused be harm,
Don't care whether I wear galoshes
For the rest of my life,
Or, what I'll have for breakfast, lunch or dinner,
And, that my motto is:
"If I'll make one good deed a day
Then it will make my day,
And, if my day turns to failure
Then it's okay,
Since, there is always the next day
To turn it all into a big success.'

And this is when their faces turned pale white,
The color of the Lily-white,
Began to sweat,
As if they held an explosive dynamite,
Their eyes began to seek for fight or flight,
And still they found a way to laugh,
But, only this time not at me,
But at themselves,

---

4       B.U. – Boston University.

Since it didn't have the sound
Of the triumphant laugh of Ha! Ha! Ha!
Instead, it sounded like wailing hyenas
From nervousness and of the tight knot
That lodged in their gut,
As if, there lay a parasite
Who was defeated by the words of light.

May, 2019

# The Only One I Miss
By Artem Vaskanyan

I've lost, and lost, and lost again.
So much has been lost in one lifetime
That there is nothing more left to lose,
In ten lifetimes from now.

What I've lost,
I don't even know
How to begin to describe it.
It is beyond the language that I speak.

When you lose someone you love,
Not only do you feel abandoned and alone
In the heart of the Black Forest;
But also torn apart to pieces
By the pack of wolves,
Who prey on helpless victims
Desolated by their loss.

And this is when you start to question
The fairness of the life and death,
And the essence of all existence
That all men find themselves
Grappling with to the end.

You seek and search to find some answers
To justify the reason for the one you lost;
And find some way to alleviate the pain
That has entombed itself deep down
Of what you used to call your soul.

And when all this fails,

You start to look for a quiet place
To escape judgmental eyes from watching;
So you can shed your tears in isolation
And cry as freely as the birds fly above your head,
And sigh the aching pain
That oozes through your pores
And swells your veins.

And somewhere in the midst of it all,
You curse the One who gave you all;
And your belief in the Creator fractures,
And scares you for the remainder of your life.

And just like that
You drift for million miles away,
Trapped in your own thoughts
Out of desperation;
And pray in silence
To the One you cursed
To help you join the loved one
Whom you have lost,
And miss the most
From all your losses.

The pain of losing the one you lost,
It overwhelms you every single moment.
It grows and gnaws at you
And pulls you down by a great distance;
Until your heart becomes as heavy as a brick,
And begins to sink to the bottom of the ocean.

And this is where it aches and burns the most,
As every thought you make
Of the one you lost;

It leaves you broken hearted and destroyed.
Without a single hope for consolation;
To repair internal wounds from desolation.

This loss has turned me inside out.
It changed me to the point
Where I will never be the same;
And left me with nothing that I consider
Is worth living for until this very day.

Oh! How I wish to see you one last time.
To hug you, kiss you,
And beg for you to stay
For just long enough to tell you;
That you are the only one
I miss and love
From all my losses.

May, 2019

# FROM NOTHING, COMES EVERYTHING
By Artem Vaskanyan

This is no place for Adam and Eve,
This is not Eden;
Here between the mountains and the valleys,
No trees grow,
No grass appears,
No seeds of any kind sprout,
Nothing can be sowed or reaped,
Only naked lifeless trees are left behind.

This is no place for Pharaohs,
This is not Valley of the King;
Here up in the sky,
No sun rays shine,
No moon glows,
No stars of any kind emerge,
Nothing can be seen as light,
Only dark clouds swirl above.

This is no place for Aristotle, Socrates or Plato,
This is not Amphitheater;
Here down on earth,
No mind expands,
No discussions occur,
No rhetoric given,
No enlightenment of any kind takes light,
Nothing can be heard, nor words uttered,
Only dead silence roams the earth.

This is no place for a living soul,
This is not Heaven, Hell or Mother Earth;
Here in the unknown realm,

No souls dwell,
No diviners guide,
No Messiahs preach,
No gods are worshipped of any kind,
Nothing can be saved or left worth saving,
Only wicked spirits are left to roam the lands.

Here, in between the sky and earth,
No oceans form,
No seas rise,
No rivers flow,
No ponds of any kind emerge;
Nothing can be found with life,
Only dried up wells are left behind.

Here, in the godforsaken lands,
No people left alive,
No animals show any sign of life.
No insects of any kind crawl to surface;
Nothing can be called living,
Only cold wind and dust spirals around.

Here, in the middle of nowhere,
No North,
No South,
No West or East exists,
Every direction looks the same;
Nothing can be located,
Only an empty void of space exists.

This is no place for actors,
This is not Theater;
Here on the "Stage",
You cannot pretend

To be someone you are not;
This place is real,
As dark clouds above my head
And terra firma under my naked feet;
This place has no pity for the weak, sick or old,
One small mistake, a wrong uttered word,
Will send you to isolation
For the remainder of your life;
Where it will become the end of you
And everything else that is left in you;
And weather you stay or leave, survive or perish,
It all depends on you;
But in either case,
No matter how you choose to live or die,
You will never be the same again;
This life will change you into something
That is completely foreign to you;
It will make you feel
Disgusted with yourself,
With whatever that is inside of you
That finds itself to dwell.

And, Yet!
Here in the middle of nowhere,
And at the same time, in the center of it all,
Deep down in a man's burning core,
Where dwells his broken soul,
No living or dead soul
Can ever bring its filth into his lonely heart.

And here, in a lifeless place,
Where naked trees are left to stand alone and rot,
His soul is always burning
With endless life and joy'

No naked, lifeless, rotten trees,
Or dried up grass are ever found;
Instead, gardens of evergreen trees and flowers
Bloom of every color,
Never lose its brightness and aroma.

And here, where dark clouds swirl above,
The Sun is (always) shining,
The Moons are (always) glowing,
The Stars are (always) burning,
The Sky is (always) clear,
As crystal clear as the water at my feet.

And here, in a lifeless place,
Where dried up wells are left behind,
The animals of every kind
Can all be seen in vivid colors,
In the garden that never disappears;
The Oceans, Seas and endless Rivers
Extend as far as gods can see;
In deserts small oasis are filled
With elixir of life,
For any living soul to come and drink
And satisfy its thirst,
And live again with joy.

And here, where cold wind and dust spirals around,
There are always people who I adore,
And worth remembering forever in my memoirs,
And cherish them in lucid dreams
That come to me when least expected
In the midst of the night.

And here, where empty void of space exists,

A space between the life and death
That I often call to be part of my life;
Is where I feel the most alive;
And, it is here, where my Heaven, Hell and Sanctuary
All come to life.

And here, where dead silence roams the earth,
In the pitch dark hole,
A man often finds himself
Sitting, praying and ruminating,
Behind closed iron doors;
His body is as naked as the lifeless tree.
His mind is as stagnant as the water can be.
The ceiling is his limit,
It is his Sky!
The walls, in all four directions are all the same,
No matter which way he turns, it all looks the same,
The void of space is in a man's mind,
Who finds himself living in a place
Where there is nowhere to go,
Nothing to see,
But a small window above his head,
Where the Sun, the Moon and Stars
All take turns to illuminate his lonely path,
And guide him to escape from this dreadful life,
And give him hope to have a better life someday.

And here, where the wicked spirits
Are left to roam the lands,
Where life is no longer equally balanced
Between the suffering and joy,
Is where people lose themselves, self-mutilate,
And even hang themselves;
Give up on life,

Like life does not even matter.

Here, in the pitch dark hole,
Deep down in a man's broken soul;
Months feel like years,
Weeks like days,
Days like hours,
Hours like minutes,
And seconds like months,
And even years at the most desperate times;
Time does not exist,
A man only thinks it does,
And it is exactly why,
A man's mind becomes lost, consumed, controlled
By the void of time;
And it is here where he hears
Screams during the day,
Silence throughout the night,
Screams throughout the day,
Dead silence during the night,
The night feels like day,
The day feels like night,
Surrounded by the chaos
Throughout Day and Night;
When silence comes,
It does not come from calm or peaceful life,
But from exertion of an agonizing life,
And godforsaken, cold, lifeless place,
A man often calls his only home.

Here, there is no future to think about,
No past to dwell upon,
No present to hold on,
And, Yet!

A man always finds a way
To think of them all,
All at the same time.

Here, a man owns nothing,
Nothing belongs to him,
Not even his breath,
Even that he must give back;
A man owns nothing in this world,
He only thinks he does,
A lie that had been told
Since his early creation,
Out of confusion and misinterpretation
By the ones who claim to know the word of God.

And, Yet!
When silence comes,
It is when least expected;
And when it does, it spreads like night,
Consuming every gleam of light
Without pity in its path,
Nor choosing whose good or bad;
And when it is here, it is everywhere,
It becomes the language of God.

This silence, it is the voice of God,
That cannot be seen or heard,
But only felt with every burning atom
That dwells inside in every man,
Who have been desolated by despair, pain,
And from constant misery of life.

This silence! This voice of God!
It penetrates a man deep down to its core,

To the marrow of his cold bones,
Where it invigorates his soul,
Brings him back to life
And gives him back what he had lost;

It puts him in a place
Where he can forge his soul,
Become his own Pharaoh, King
And even God, in his own mind;
Hear Messiahs' parables,
Follow Deviners' teachings,
And start his path with a new beginning;
And it even makes it more profound,
In a man who had never felt a drop of joy.

This silence! This voice of God!
It turns the swamp back into a pond,
And lets it flow like a river into the seas,
And from there expands into the oceans
As far as gods can see;
And it is here,
Where everything comes back to life,
Where from nothing, comes everything in life.

May, 2019

# If You Can't Let Go

By Artem Vaskanyan

If you can't let go
Of what had been said
And done to you,
Then you must find the courage
To let go
Of the person who had said it,
And done it to you.

And, if you can't let go
Of them both,
Then prepare yourself to suffer
From carrying the burden
Of them both.

June, 2019

# She Is Beautiful!

By Artem Vaskanyan

She is beautiful!
This much is true,
But is she as beautiful on the inside
As she is on the outside?
That is the real question that I grapple with, -
For it is only God knows
What truly lurks deep down inside her heart.

I know this much though,
That with time her external beauty will fade away,
And then the only part that will remain
Is the internal side
Which lurks deep down inside
That which she had gathered throughout her life;

And since, I am one of those
Who is more attracted to the internal beauty,
The kindness, intelligence and above all her understanding,
Rather than to her external beauty;

Thus, I always look as close as I can
In hopes to see what truly dwells
Deep down inside that heart.

June, 2019

# THE SPIRIT OF THE GRAY WOLF
By Artem Vaskanyan

In me, lives the spirit of the gray wolf,
And not of some wild dog.
In me, every fiber of my body
Wants to jump up and run, and howl
At the first site of the full moon.
And, even though, I wasn't born in wilderness
The wilderness was born in me.
It makes me feel connected to the Mother Nature,
And see the sky, as my father,
The earth, as my mother,
And the stars, as my ancestors
Whose blood flow through my veins.

A man has no way to predict
Which spirit will come and bind with his soul.
Since, all mankind are born with the spirit
Who chooses them as its own vessel
Way before they are even born.

Some spirits have the power
To make you fly,
And some to make you crawl,
Some spirits are strong,
And some are weak.
Some can withstand control,
Oppression, chaos in your life,
And some break at the first sign
Of hardship in your life.
Some spirits possess great consciousness
To perceive,
Of their own thoughts and behaviors.

The spirit of the gray wolf,
The one that lives in me,
It has its weaknesses
And it has its strengths.
But, the best part of it
Is that it's always free,
To ask and question everything in life,
And see the mystery of secular and celestial life
As clearly as the night owl sees its prey
In the pitch dark forest night
Where everyone else is blind to see
And lost between two worlds.
One that pertains to men
And the other two spirits.

There must be a good reason why?
A spirit binds itself to a particular human's soul,
And to the vessel that it chooses to possess
Before a man is born.

Perhaps, the mystery of the celestial beings
Weren't meant for just any man to know.
Perhaps, not every question can be answered
That men grapples with.
Perhaps it's best to leave
The mystery of the celestial beings
To the spirits in the spiritual realm,
And the earthly mysteries to a man.
And, perhaps the spirit of the gray wolf,
The one that lives in me,
Is as bewildered as any other soul
That dwells around me.

June, 2019

# My Dear Friend
By Artem Vaskanyan

My friend, my friend, my dear friend,
Where have you been?
What have you done?
You haven't even changed a bit,
But only your appearance did.

It's truly been a long time
For both of us,
Since we've seen each other
This up close.

I'm glad to see you.
I really am!
And, it's good to be here with you again.
And maybe even
I'll hear from you again?
This time much sooner than I hope.

I'm sorry, I haven't called or wrote
As often as you wanted.
I couldn't bring myself
To bother you from hell.
Why should I be the one
To remind you of this wretched life
That you once had with me in hell.

Perhaps one day we'll meet again.
And, if not in person
Then at least from far away.
And, if not in this life
Then in the next for sure.

But, overall, I think
It's for the best this way.
Since, it seems to me
That I've caused nothing but pain
To you and those
Who were once close to me.

When you had left,
I still could feel the presence
Of your spirit here with me.
And in the places where we once walked
And shared our soulful conversations,
And most soul-draining moments of our lives,
I saw your spirit's shadow pass through before my eyes.

And, heard the presence say,

My friend, my friend, my dear friend,
Where have you been?
What have you done?
You haven't even changed a bit,
But only your appearance did, -

July, 2019

# Tonight We'll Feast!

By Artem Vaskanyan

Tonight we'll feast!
Tonight we'll celebrate the love
Between two of our beloved children,
Who will become united by the grace of God
Under the same naked sky
As our ancestors had
Done so for millenniums;

And feel the presence of both gods,
Of Vishnu, protector of the world,
And, of Jesus, son of God;
Whose love will radiate
And build the bond.
Between two distinct families
By culture, traditions and religion.

Tonight we'll feast!
Tonight our glasses will be filled with wine
And raised above our heads,
To catch the light
From the glowing moon and stars,
And give a toast to our beloved children,
To have a happy and long life.

Tonight we'll feast!
Tonight we'll taste the food
From many distinct cultures,
And drink the sweetest wines
That we preserved in our cellars
For a special moment to arrive;

And, so we'll drink,
And eat, and drink again,
Until our bellies are filled with food and wine,
And ready to burst from a good laughter.

Tonight we'll feast!
Tonight we'll dance to the chamber music
Played by the hired instrumentalists,
As loud as the noise of the friendly crowd;
Whose voices will be heard,
As they will echo through
Every corner of the wedding yard;

And as both of these elegant
And graceless sounds
Continue through the night,
They will merge together
And become one sweet sound
From which we'll hear many different stories
About the past, the present and the future lives
Of bride and groom;

And, of how they both look so beautifully together,
Like they were meant to find each other,
As one finds a needle in a haystack,
Not out of luck,
But out of fate
For some unknown, chosen task;

And this is when we'll notice
In the depth of the jubilant crowd
Both fathers and mothers of the bride and groom
Overwhelmed with joy within their heart.
And full of glowing smiles on the outside;

Except for deep inside their soul
Will lurk a hidden drop of doubt
That simply just can't disappear
From some brief moment of pure joy,
Since, it doesn't know
How to let go,
Of their precious one.

Tonight we'll feast!
Tonight we'll toast and sing of our mothers,
Tell courageous stories of our fathers,
And remember the rest of our ancestors
Who are no longer here with us;

And somewhere amongst those words,
We'll than our God!
For giving us the blessing
To live, to love, and share
Our happiness with one another,
And celebrate together
Amongst our family and friends
The love between two of our beloved children.

Salute! We'll yell,
And clinch our crystal glasses full of wine
With those within our reach,
To resonate a ringing sound
For a dramatic sound effect,
To make ourselves feel important in some way;
And in the process, deliberately or not,
Spill a little bit of wine
On the table and on the ground,
And quickly raise our glasses to our lips
To acquiesce with the toast,

And seal the deal,
By making sure our glasses drained
To its last drop,
To honor names of people
Of whom our elders had spoken upon;

And then we'll slam our empty crystal glasses
Directly on the table's yellow curtain
Stained with circles of rosy colors
From spilled red wine;
And yell, more wine!
For sommeliers to come,
And fill our empty glasses up
With sweet red wine again.

And just like that
We'll eat, drink, sing and dance
Throughout the rest of the wedding night.

July, 2019

# THE PHOTOGRAPH
By Artem Vaskanyan

I wish I had a photograph of you!
So, I could compare myself to you;
And see it for myself,
If I turned out to be like you.

Long time ago,
Way before I learned how to even walk,
I caught a glimpse of a photograph of you;
By picking through old photos
In my mother's shoe-box that she hid
Under the giant divan;

But then, the next think I remember, [thing]
I see it torn to pieces
Before my own two eyes,
And thrown like trash
Into the flames of a fire place
By my own dear mother;
Where I watched it curled up,
Turned to smoke and burned to ashes
By unbiased flames;

And as I watched with frozen tears in my eyes,
The only thing that I could think about was,
What color of the eyes and hair you had.

I guess when she got remarried
Five years after your sudden death,
She had decided all by herself
To forget the life
That she once had with you

And the two sons that she had bore for you.
(How inconsiderate it was of you,
To only think of no one else but you!)

I searched so hard
To find another photograph of you,
But as of yet,
Not a single image of your face
Had been saved by anyone I ever knew.

(When you so shamelessly tore to pieces
The last photograph,
And threw it in the flames of fire
To be devoured pitilessly,
Not only did you erase
The only image of my father's face;
But you had also turned your back
On the only man you ever knew
Who shared his life and gave his heart
Wholeheartedly to you).

(You tried so adamantly
To erase him from my memory
With your vicious lies,
And by telling me
That your new husband was
My real father
And the only man you ever knew;
But I always knew
Deep down in my aching heart
That none of it was true);

(And not just because,
There was never a real love

Between the "father" and the son right from the start),
But because of the photograph of you
That till this day lingers in my heart.

(To erase the existence of the father
From your son's memory,
It is the same as to make him die again!)

(I wish you would've never discarded so negligently
The only photograph I ever loved,
Nor told some lies so stubbornly
That in the end, all it ever did
Was to cause me doubt
In everything else you ever said).

(Perhaps, if right from the start
You would've been honest with me,
We would've never lived so far apart
And maybe even would've had a better life).

The Photograph would've never brought me closure
From not having a chance to meet with you,
But it would've answered many questions
That till this day
I keep asking about you;
(And, it would've given me a lesser reason,
Not to live so far away from you).

August, 2019

# An Old Man And His Judas
By Artem Vaskanyan

An old man once told me about his Judas,
And this is what he said:

"It pinched my soul and broke my heart
To see a man whom I used to call my friend,
To take a stand at the witness box
In a court of law,
And point his finger in my face
Without any shame,
Or respect for either one of us;

"It took me by surprise,
Not of what he said
But the way he said it;
Incriminating me for everything
That he did himself;

"These dirty words
That he had twisted in his favor
Has hurt me deeper than he thinks;
It made me lose the trust
In all man-kind,
And think of the world
As a dark forsaken place;

"It ripped the breath right out of me,
When I realized what he had done to me;
Betrayed, is not even enough
To describe the way I felt
When I heard these filthy words
That send me to the slammer

For the remainder of my life;

"In truth!
I don't even think he fully realized
What he had done,
When he sold me down the river
For the price, as to avoid
By going to the same damned place
To where he himself so gladly helped those
Who wanted to see me crucified on the cross;

"What he has done,
Was much more than just betray me;
He has also betrayed his own poor soul,
And changed his name
From what his mom had called him,
Since the beginning of his time,
To Judas!
Which now will be the only name
That people will call him by;

"From now on, he will be known as a man
Who chose to simplify his life and ease his pain
At the expense of inflicting more upon another;
For the despicable crime
That he had also done himself,
And yet,
Instead of being punished, got rewarded;

"For the harm that he had caused,
His Judas' soul was cursed
With a mark of shame engraved into his soul;
For him to bare,
Until he will become an empty man,

An empty vessel,
Torn apart by his own poor soul;

"No matter where he goes,
No matter what he does or says,
His wicked actions and his vile words
Will be recognized from a mile away,
By any man with a moral soul;

"Because of his immoralistic ways,
He has converted to Judasism;
Where the sole practice of this religion
Is to betray people who are close to him,
For any profit that may appear suitable to him;

"For many years that I had been away,
In a place as dark as blindness;
All I felt was hate,
And thought of nothing but revenge for him;

"This loathe, this revolting vengeance
That I felt for him,
It felt like a burning furnace
Was ripping through my chest,
And all it ever did was
To fuel my heart with hatred;

"And even though, at times,
It was the only reason
That gave me motivation
And strength to overcome another day,
And in the process orchestrate my devious plan,
When, how, and where to take revenge on him;

"And yet, at the end of the day,
It gnawed away the only parts of me
That wanted to forgive
For what my Judas had done to me;

"Ever since his vile words were heard,
My heart has never been the same;
And this is why up to this day,
I consider him to be much worse
Than the Judas himself;
Since, he at least was seized
With some remorse,
When he realized what he had done was wrong;

"But not my Judas, he was something else,
Something that I just couldn't comprehend;
Perhaps the only way for me
To truly grasp his Judas way,
Was to convert to Judasism
That I abhor with all my heart,
Till this day;

"In truth!
I would rather be crucified again,
Than to become a man who sells his soul
And brings nothing but chaos and demise
Upon another poor man's soul;

"I always thought as I laid in the dark hole,
Engulfed in my own deep thoughts,
That the only way to rectify his treachery
Was to help him find his Judas' tree,
And watch him do what Judas did
When he found his tree;

And hanged, until his body decomposed,
And spilled the guts in the field of blood;[5]

"But then, it dawned suddenly on me,
As it came in silent whisper from within my soul,
And put me in a trance to make me see
That it is not up to me,
To judge and take revenge on him;

"To cause him the same pain
That I had felt by his wicked hand,
Would mean that I
Would have to become like him;
The same Judas whom I have cursed,
Until I ended up,
At the lowest point in my life;

"and so it hit me
Like lightning strikes a tree,
And cleared my clouded mind
Like a fog disperses from the woods
By a gentle breeze;
That revenge is in the Creator's hands,
It has nothing to do with me."

August, 2019

---

5       From Acts 1:18. Field of Blood, a place where Judas hanged him-
self.

# A SYCAMORE TREE
By Artem Vaskanyan

It was in the midst of the summer,
And in the middle of the day;
The sun was blazing heat from all directions
And the air was muggy and difficult to breathe,
The trees stood still unshaken by the breeze
And all the life around me felt as if it died.

A crow as black as night appeared in the sky
And gently landed on the lifeless tree,
And began to caw religiously,
As a reminder to me, and all the people around me
That we're being watched.

I stood just far enough to see, an open black casket
Where his dead body laid peacefully
Under the scorching sun.

It wasn't my first time,
Since I've seen a dead man in front of me;
But it was my first,
To attend a funeral of a dead friend of mine.

I couldn't bring myself to take another step
To pay respect to him, face to face,
Like any decent friend should've done;
And not because, I struggled to accept the fact
That he was gone,

But because of the young grieving mother
Who sat by his side,
With a black cloak rapped around her neck,

And rhythmically swayed back and forth,
As she beat her chest with an open hand
And with the other tore her long-gray hair,
And wailed wildly with tears pouring
Down her exhausted face,
And with her worn out eyes,
She stared at the lifeless body,
And then looked up into the blazing sun
With a pleading gaze to bring him back,
And then stared back at her son's face,
In hopes to see a change.

And there, under the same merciless sun,
By her side, sat, the same age as once was her son,
A teenage boy with murky tears in his eyes,
Who begged forgiveness with his pleading hands
And pointless words,
For putting her only son into that casket
Where he'll remain from now on;

And behind them both stood a pastor from their church,
Dressed in a black suit and tie,
And with a sinister expression in his eye, made known
That he had orchestrated this forceful act of forgiveness,
Between the grieving mother and a teenage boy,
Who became a man when he drove her son to meet his doom.

A gentle breeze suddenly turned into a violent wind
And blew vigorously at my back;
My feet moved swiftly forth, not by choice,
But by some unknown force that pushed me from behind;
I felt a sudden chill pass down to my spine,
And only then when I approached, did the gloomy picture
Unravel and come to life before my eyes;

'A reality of life,
That at any moment,
And at any given time,
Life can cease to exist,
In a blink of an eye.'

And this is when I saw disfigured face
And stitched wounds around his swollen head,
From going through, head first,
Out of the back windshield of a car
That a young man, who, is now sitting
By his mother's side, drove into a tree
And split the car down the middle, into two halves,
Like an axe splits a piece of wood
With one short stroke.

The driver and the older sister of a dead friend
Both miraculously cheated death,
But not him! Not my friend!
His fate was sealed by the Death itself
Who awaited him in the shape of a sycamore tree
By the side of the road that looked like
A twisted serpent trapped in the dense forest.

When he fell to his doom,
Every bone from head to toe shattered like a glass,
And as he laid, twisted like a snake,
In the middle of the road,
Blood poured from his eyes, ears and mouth,
And the Death stared in this face.

Before his eyes where drained of light,
His sister dropped right by his side
To her naked knees in the pool of blood,

And begged him to stay with her under the moon light;

He tried to leave her with last words,
But all that came out was a short wheeze
Without any last words.

August, 2019

# JUST ANOTHER DREAM

By Artem Vaskanyan

I haven't been myself lately.
Not since that day,
When I woke up in the middle of the night
With a disgusting feeling in my gut,
Like someone gutted me with a rusted knife
And pulled my viscera right out of me,
Like I was some kind of fish
Who got caught for taking a bite off
Of something that didn't belong to me.

A nightmare, I thought it was at first,
But it was not,
Since, everything that happened in my dream
To its last drop of blood,
It all was real;

*except*
Accept for one small part,
Where it wasn't I who bled that blood,
But some unknown guy
Whom I've briefly seen,
Before another gutted him
Like I've never seen.

I wish I wasn't there to witness this horror flick,
And wouldn't be,
If I wasn't surrounded by four (brick) walls,
A metal (barred) door
That I don't have a key to,
And a watchdog,
Who guards the main gate around the clock.

I know it was just another dream,
But after all the violence that I've seen,
I'm just glad that I didn't end up
Like that guy with the rusted knife,
Or the other who lost his guts.

August, 2019

# A Good Advice

By Artem Vaskanyan

I know things about life, and what to do or not
In awkward situations;

I know about relationships between a man and a woman,
And especially how to get out of one
Without being called a dick;

I know about love and hate, forgiveness and revenge,
Pleasure and suffering, and above all compassion;

And I even know a thing or two
About the teachings of the Buddha;

But the best thing out of all that I know about best,
Is how to give a good advice,
To any person of any age, race and gender;

And this is what I advise:

When you see someone who is
Full of hate, revenge and suffering,
Show indifference.
When you see someone who is
Full of pleasure, hate and revenge,
Show indifference in a pleasant way.
When you see someone who is
Full of forgiveness, pleasure, and hate,
Show indifference in a forgiving and pleasant way.
And, when you see someone who is
Full of love, forgiveness and pleasure,
Then find a right moment to show compassion.

August, 2019

# Broken Heart

By Artem Vaskanyan

When darkness fills a broken heart
And light has lost its glow,
The only thing then left to do
Is hope for a better day to come through.

For when the light loses its glow,
And nothing in life
Starts to make sense,
Then, hope becomes the only salvation
To reignite the flickered out light
That has been fractured by devastation.

For hope, isn't hope,
Nor light, is light'
Unless it's the last thing
That a broken heart holds on to
For its dear life.

For where the hope is found,
So is the light
Emerges instantly from the dark
To heal its broken heart.

For light cannot be felt or seen,
Unless, it's surrounded
By the total darkness.

For darkness cannot exist without the light,
Nor light without the darkness;
They are both bound to one another,
Just like a broken heart and hope

Intertwined forever with one another.

October, 2019

# A Ghost, Roaming
### By Artem Vaskanyan

Sometimes I feel like I'm a ghost, roaming.
Not belonging to one specific place,
People, culture, tradition, language, religion, -
For I have lived and experienced them all
Too broadly for too long;

That even now, I still feel that I have lost
All senses of my belonging,
For I no longer feel nostalgic, bound
To one special place;

For I'm like a wind without a home,
And a constant flowing river
That never stagnates in one place;

For my mind is like a waterfall
That never ceases to cascade,
But my soul,
It craves for a pond
So that one day
I'll be stagnant like a home.

October, 2019

# Dipsomania*

By Artem Vaskanyan

Last night you saw me shed my tears
For the first time.

Embarrassed I feel today,
For I cannot even dare
To look you in your eyes.

But not yesterday,
Not last night,
For I was someone else,
Or more like something else
That even I did not recognize.

Forgive me for my devilish behavior,
For I was not myself last night;

My dipsomania had once again
Dominated my inner-self.

It worked on me, as usually,
Like a truth serum;

Forcing me to reveal
My deepest-darkest secrets
About myself to you.

I know it was the spirits
That gave me courage to open up
My can of worms;

And spill what I had suppressed

For as long as I can remember-

For I was too ashamed
To share my deepest-darkest secrets
And not being understood,
The true reason for my devilish behavior
When my dipsomania
Dominates my inner-self.

And so,
Now you know;

What makes me sad,
What drive me mad,
What breaks my heart,
What heals my soul,
What gives me hope,
What wins my love,
What makes me talk
And shed tears,
In the midst of the night
When you and I are alone.

October, 2019

* An insatiable craving for alcoholic beverages.

# ÉMIGRÉ[6]

By Artem Vaskanyan

For I have left, seeing that my political conditions
No longer matched the status of my permanent residence
In the place where I was born.

This I know now, but then, it was confusing, Mind-Boggling
To my ignorant seven-year-old mind;

For I was a citizen of a country, brought into life by birth
On the land that I, once upon a time so proudly called my home.

Up to a moment, when I became cognizant that I could not
Even be forcefully deported from my long captivity
In the foreign land, north East facing the Atlantic Ocean,[7]
Back to my homeland, West Asia overlooking the Caspian Sea to
East.[8]

Never mind to even visit out of my free will,
(Not that I could due to my ongoing situation)
For I am forbidden to set foot on the land
Where I am a third generation native to my homeland.

For I am labeled as an enemy of the state
For being guilty of nothing more than being an Armenian,
Since I was seven years old.

For a long time, I felt embarrassed,
For being stigmatized by my own native land;
And torn apart between my people and my home by the

---

6       One who has left a native country, for political reasons.
7       Massachusetts, U.S.A.
8       Baku, Azerbaijan

Azerbaijani
And Armenian War[9] over the disputed land enclave of Nagorno-
Karabakh;[10]
And overwhelmed with grief for losing my childhood friends,
And my sense of identity, for I no longer knew
Where I was supposed to belong.

Embarrassed, overwhelmed with grief I feel no more,
For I feel great pity, for those who banished not only me,
But the entire two hundred thirty thousand of the Armenians
Out of West Asia overlooking the beautiful Caspian Sea to East.

But my nostalgia, is something beyond my control.
It never ceases, but only continues to grow heavily on my soul.

For when I left my home, so did a piece of my soul
Was left behind along with my home.

I often dream of returning back home
And recovering my abandoned piece of soul
That yearns for my return to reconnect with my shattered soul.

Thinking back, now it all makes perfect sense.
Why I was suddenly put on the train with my anoush Mayrig,[11]
With one way ticket from Baku to Armavir[12] and sent up North
Passing through the Caucasus Mountains and leaving behind
The beautiful Caspian Sea to the East, to never return to it again,
But only in the distant dream that comes to take me back
When I feel homesick.

9       War of 1988-94; an official cease fire signed in 1994
10      A region in Azerbaijan where 94% of the people are Arme-
nian.
11      Sweet Mother (Armenian)
12      (Baku) capital of Azerbaijan; (Armavir) capital of the Providence
   Krasnodar, USSR; Union of Soviet Socialist Republics

There was no option! There was no time to waste! But emigre,
Or perish by the same neighbors' hands with whom we shared
The same land for a so many generations, and whose animosity
for us
Has grown stronger with each day by the spread of the Azerbaijani
Government's propaganda.

To avoid becoming a casualty of war, we left,
Or more like ran for our dear lives, but not before,
We tried to sell what we could manage.

our     favorite?

Or sofa, my favored divan, where so many memories were left
Etched forever in my mind;

It brings to mind when I used to climb on top of the cabinet,
Calling from the top of my lungs, for my Dédushka and
Bábushka[13]
To step into the bedroom and watch me do a somersault
From the top of the cabinet onto divan.

— the divan?

So I could see my Bábushka laugh and my Dédushka yell,
Calling me Khent Sumashétshiy![14] Mixing his Armenian with
Russian
To stress his frustration, as he would storm out of the room
With his hands behind his back and his head shaken out of
disappointment.

And not to mention my enormous Black-piano where I spent
Countless hours playing or more like making noise to be frank.

And our two bedroom apartment each with decent sized balcony
Opposite of one another; one overlooking our neighborhood

13      Grandfather and Grandmother (Russian)
14      Crazy (Armenian/Russian)

yard

_watching_

Where I would find my Bábushka sitting and watch over me like
a hawk,
As I played with my dear friends in the neighborhood yard;
And the other, overlooking the women's prison where I would
spend hours,
Upon hours sitting on a balcony floor staring with my piercing
gaze
At the prison's window bars from across the street, in hope to see
Some movement, some sign of life.

This War!
This Exile!
This Banishment!
This Turmoil!
This Forced Migration!
Effected not only mine, but all Armenian families
Throughout the regions of Azerbaijan.

And many families just like mine were prevented to withdraw
Their life savings from the National Bank of Azerbaijan.
For it became forbidden to service any person
With an Armenian name or even origin.

Nor could we sell our life's possessions for a decent price,
For many Azerbaijani neighbors who claimed to be our friends
For many generations, not only turned their backs on us,
But turned to vultures out of greed to capitalize on our despaired
Urgency to leave and in the process leave our property behind,
So they could get it all for gratis.

And those who did offer, offered offensive prices;
1 Kopek[15] on the Ruble.

---

15      (Kopeika) a coin equal to 1/100 of the Russian Ruble.

Offended by these ridiculous amounts, many destroyed their
Life's possessions with their bare hands,
Than see it fall into the hands of their oppressors.

But amongst those vultures there were some true friends
Who stayed loyal to the end and helped their lifelong friends
With whom they celebrated countless Birthdays! Holidays!
And shared their livelihood since we could remember.

These true life friends have helped to safely emigrate
Despite the fact that they were scared for their lives;

For if they were to get caught in any form or shape
Then they too would find themselves labeled as the enemy of
the state,
And be imprisoned or even worse, perish without a chance
emigrer;
For Traitors were treated much worse than us.

After we emigrated from our homes, the neighborhoods, the
schools,
The markets, the towns, the cities and the entire regions
Of the West Asia overlooking the Caspian Sea to the East
All became one cultured country.

For when we emigrated, so did the other minor nationalities
Pertaining to the Soviet people followed our footsteps.

What once was known as a vivacious region became a ghost place
Of nothing more than memories of where once the Armenians
And many other Soviet people lived and kept these places
Full of spirit, full of life with their traditions, cultures,
Languages and social views, and all that was needed
To live a long, happy and peaceful life.

December, 2019

# THE DANCING FLAMES OF PYRO[16]
By Artem Vaskanyan

It's been ages,
Since I felt the real heat and light
From the dancing flames of Pyro
On my hands and face.

It sure feels nice,
Especially the heat on my cold face,
For it's winter outside
And it's the middle of the night
Where I'm not the only life
That is fighting to survive.

For all the creatures of the night
That are hidden from the light
In deep shadows of the night
That growl and howl behind my back,
Lack the spirit to come to light;

For dancing flames of Pyro
Are not for just any living being to face,
They are too powerful
For just anyone to stare directly in their face.

It sure smells good,
The burning cherry firewood
That I've thrown upon the campfire,
A sacrifice to Pyro, in exchange,
For keeping me warm with his heat and light
Throughout the cold winter night.

---

16      Fire (Greek)

The smoke's aroma smells so good,
That I can taste it in my mouth.
And as I inhale it more and more,
It fills my lungs,
Until I can't breathe no more.

My head begins to spin,
Like I've taken a heavy dose of heroin,
And fall into a trance.

Inside my core,
The heat begins to rise,
And I profusely drip with sweat,
Like I'm trapped once again
Inside the sweat box,[17]

My eyes open wide,
They don't blink but stare directly
Into the dancing flames of Pyro
And see his face;

And in his face, I see his soulful eyes,
And in his soulful eyes, I see the nature of his soul,
And within his soul, I see my face;

And in my face, I see my soulful eyes,
And in my soulful eyes, I see the nature of my soul,
And within my soul, I see his soul,
And how his soul is free
From burden to survive,
Nor showing concern how he would live or die;

---

17     A cell with a high temperature in which a prisoner is placed as a
punishment.

For he surrendered the essence of his life
To the Creator,
And in return, was granted eternal life.

In this cold winter night,
I'm bound to Pyro more than to any other life
That I've ever come to know
Throughout my entire life.

For my life depends on his survival
To keep me warm throughout the night
And so does his on mine,
For it's I who feed him to stay alive.

We're no different from one another,
For he's just like me,
Breathes air and feeds to stay alive
Throughout this cold winter night.

I sacrifice another cherry firewood
Into the dying flames of Pyro,
And in exchange,
I see him joyfully spring back to life
From the embers of the fire;

And perform a dazzling dance
As he begins to rise
And grow higher, higher, higher,
Until his sparkling, dancing flames
Blend in with the gazillion brilliant stars
And dissipate into the clear sky of the universe.

December 31, 2019

# SITTING IN THE HOUSE
By Artem Vaskanyan

Sitting in the house of someone
I barely know,
And through the stranger's window,
I look up to the sky,
And can't see a single star
Known to my eyes.

Sitting, drinking, and singing to myself
And watching two cougars dance
In front of me;

To be frank!
They're not my type,
For one of them is too damn skinny
And misses a front tooth;

And the other is too damn thick
With a colossal schnozzle on her face;

Besides, they both look too Bitchy
On their faces,
And act like two starving vultures
Hovering over a lovely flower.

I pour myself a drink
With no ice,
And feel the burn
Pass through my chest;

I pour another in
And send it down

To meet its friend;

I drink and drink,
Until I can't feel my face
And barely hold an empty bottle
In my hand;

sitting in the HoUsE
of someone i've known all my LiFe,
and through my BeSt FrIeNd'S WiNdOw
i look up to the SkY,
and see all the StArS
known to my EyEs;

sTaNdInG, EaTiNg, and SiNgInG
to my FrIeNdS,
and DaNcInG with the two most BeAuTiFuL
gOdDeSsEs that i have ever SeEn;

to be StRaIgHt Up!
they are most DeFiNiTeLy my TyPe;

for they have AmAzInG FiGuReS,
lOvElY SmIlEs,
and both look too AmOrOuS
in their FaCeS;

besides, they act like two GoRgEoUs DoVeS
hovering over an UgLy CoRpSe.

January 1, 2020

# THE SOLO ODYSSEY OF LIFE
### By Artem Vaskanyan

The solo odyssey of life
Is one giant mystery.

No one knows
To where one truly goes
Not even till the end of days.

The journey never ceases to go on,
Not as long as there is a heart beat
And the flow of life
Continues to exist in a mortal life.

The voyage has always been
More of a spiritual one
Than of a physical;

For every journey becomes a spiritual path
From constant turmoil in one's life.

Along the journey
The hidden mysteries are revealed
To make a mortal see
That the worst that could happen
At the end of each day
Is for a man to remain exactly the same
As he started his day.

The motif of the voyage
Is the selfish one
In its own way;

For when a man becomes aware
Of his self-destructive ways,
He turns into the seeker
And sets out
On the lonely quest
To cultivate his mind,
And in the process
Develops a virtuous way of life;

For virtue is
What liberates the free spirit
From the crippled life.

There is much more to life
That what the seeker
Has been told
All of his life;

And It's only through
The solo odyssey of life
That the seeker can realize
What truly is
Missing in his life.

The hardest part of
The solo odyssey of life
Has always been
And always will be
To let go of
One's old life.

The lonely voyage of life
Requires that a man
Gets out of his comfort zone,

And welcome all
Internal and external pain
Inflicted by
The solo odyssey alone.

There is no escape,
No easy way
To go through a mortal's life;

And not be exposed
To the constant pain;

For the lonely journey is engraved
In each and every living soul
From the first moment of seeing light.

The solo odyssey of life
Was never meant
To be an easy one;

For an easy journey
Does not change a soul
From worse to better,
But instead, it only changes
From worse to worst.

The sooner one
Comes to light
With an inescapable
Solo odyssey in one's life,
The sooner one
Will embrace and set out
On the lonely path
With an open mind.

January 7, 2020

# TRUE LOVE
By Artem Vaskanyan

All my life family and friends
Tried to change me,
While at the same time
Telling me that they love me;

But, if they truly love me
Then why do they try so hard
To change the way I am?

For if they truly truly love me,
Then they would've accepted me,
The way I am;

If people can't love me
For the way I am,
Then they don't really love,
They only think they do;

And they only do,
Because they've been told
All of their lives,
"To love who is close to you:"

But never truly understanding why:
Or what?
True love is.

If family and friends can't accept me
For the way I am,
Then they don't deserve
To have me in their lives.

For to mold forcefully someone,
That you think you love,
In your own image
Is not love!

But a narcissistic act
To see yourself
In the one you think you love.

For true love is truly blind
In its own way,
It doesn't see you as,
Good or bad, Ugly or beautiful, strong or weak,

But embraces you
The way you are,
Without trying to change
A single thing;

For true love!
Sees only love,
Even when it's not.

January 8, 2020

# I HAVEN'T PRAYED . . .

By Artem Vaskanyan

I haven't prayed today or yesterday,
Nor did I pray a week ago,
Or even a month;

To be frank, I can't recall
The last time when I poured out
My whole heart and soul.

My life has finally been good to me.
In fact, it has been so good
That I had no need
To drop to my knees,
Place my hands upon my heart,
Look up towards the Heaven
And pray, beg and cry;

Until, I feel the hopelessness in me is gone,
And a sense of my belonging
Is instilled in me once again.

I haven't prayed today,
Not yet, but I'm about to;

For my heart feels too heavy from the life
That I so desperately craved all my life,
But now that I do have exactly what I wanted,
I do not —

For my life became too empty,
Too easy, easy to forget
That without You!

My life makes no sense.

January 10, 2020

# THE SUMMIT
By Artem Vaskanyan

Who planted a walnut seed by the river
Hundreds of years ago? I wonder!
As I began to climb the fully grown walnut tree
To see if I could reach the heavens with my eyes
And what the world is, from above,

It must be hundreds of feet high
For it reaches the clouds in the sky.

I hugged a colossal trunk
And kissed the bark for luck
As I pushed myself up,
Until I could reach the nearest branch,
And pulled myself farther up onto a branch.

I hopped from one to another
And began to climb farther –

I climb, and see the ants climbing up with me
Without fear in their eyes to fall to their doom;
But not me –

I climb, and see the sun
Shining through the rustling leaves, .
And clouds moving swiftly through the sky
By nature's breeze.

My knees shake and I lose balance on my feet;

My hands tremble and I lose my grip;

My stomach churns and I see a blur;

My body freezes and I visualize myself falling –

I pray in silence,
To overcome my fear of falling to my doom
And that the nature's breath would ease;

I breathe, and hear the folks cheer my name
From beneath my feet,
And I find the courage to move on;

And as I climb, I stop and pick two walnut fruits,
And crack one open with another in my palms,
And eat a seed of the seed
That had been planted by some unknown being,

I climb, and see a crow's empty nest
That had been ravaged by a predator of the night,
And a bushy-tailed rodent swiftly hopped
From twig to twig,
And disappeared into a branch beneath my feet;

I climb relentlessly to reach
The highest peak of the walnut tree
So that I could see,
What the higher being must see
When he or she looks down upon me,
From above its own walnut tree;

I climb, and reach the summit of the tree
From where I look and see;

A dozen ponds where I have swam and fished,

And now they look as puddles in the grass;
The river by the side which I have crossed
A dozen times, now looks as a serpent
Crawling in the sand;

A dense forest where I would disappear to for hours,
Now looks as untidy grass;

And all the houses, cabins and barns
That surrounds the walnut tree,
Looks as dollhouses were placed
By a higher being's hand on the open field;

I look beneath my feet, and see
The ordinary folks like me
Who now all look like ants to me;

Who stare back at me, and see
What ants must see
When they look back at me,
A higher being above their heads;

I look, and see a raven hovering above my height
And she stares directly in my eyes,
And I feel free!
For I dare to stare right back
Directly in her eyes,
For I am on the same level as is she;

I see what people from beneath me cannot see,
Unless they climb
And reach the summit just like me;

For life appears much clearer now,

Not from where I stand,
But from the relentless climb
Without giving up.

January 14, 2020

# THE FORGOTTEN ONES

By Artem Vaskanyan

Who nowadays speaks of the forgotten ones,
Whose lives have been ravaged
By the genocidal hands of their oppressors.

Genocide was one of the first words
That I learned before I could even walk,
Expressed to me quite vividly by my grandparents
And regurgitated back at me
Throughout my young years by my mother
Over and over, and over . . .

And over again, of how our people, the Armenians,
Descended from the ancient tribes
Since prehistoric times,
Before even Noah's ark landed on Mount Ararat,
Had endured atrocities, mass deportations and genocides
By the Persians, Arabs and particularly
The Turks for millenniums;

And how our land became soaked with our people's blood
And carved up piece by piece starting with the Romans
Before the time of Jesus,
And after Jesus, force to convert to Christianity
In the year of 301 AD,
And abandon our Pagan religion;

And how Muslim Kurds and Turks
Stole beautiful Armenian girls from their homes
And sold them into slavery;

Violated Armenian women and murdered men

Who tried to defend their families;

Arrested, deported and executed Armenian intellectuals
For the fear that they would reveal the truth
About the Young Turks,[18] whose genocidal crimes
Caused over one and a half million innocent Armenians blood
To be spilled at the beginning of the WWI;

And how my grandfather's mother
Watched her uncles, aunts and cousins slaughtered
By the genocidal hands of the Turks and Kurds,
Barely escaping the same fate herself
From Turkey to Armenia, and then migrating to Azerbaijan
For a safer Life;

And how all Armenian historical names were excluded,
Erased from all the books, maps, streets and towns,
And replaced by the Turkish names instead;

And how till this day,
The Turkish government won't even acknowledge
That the genocide has ever taken place;

But that it was only a civil war
Between the Armenians and the Turks,
And everything else is Armenian propaganda;

How can we not speak of the forgotten ones,
Whose blood has soaked our lands,
And look each other in the eyes,
And speak of forgiveness on behalf of our oppressors

18    A member of a Turkish reformist and nationalist par-
ty, was a dominant political party in Turkey in the period of
1908 – 1918.

Who won't even acknowledge their genocidal crimes.

Who nowadays speaks of the forgotten ones,
Of the Indigenous (Native American) nations,
Whose lives have been ravaged
By the genocidal hands of their oppressors;

Who nowadays speaks of the ninety-five percent
Of the Indigenous peoples who had been wiped out
By the Spaniards, Portuguese and European-Americans
From the Americas land;

And how their lands had been taken from them,
Stripped of their cultures,
And languages, religion and rituals outlawed,
Forced to convert to Christianity, Catholicism,
Speak the language of their oppressors,
Change their appearances, be beaten, raped,
Have Native young girls sterilized without their knowledge;

Be psychologically crippled, brainwashed,
Through generations, generations upon generations,
Over and over again,
Forced mass deportations to barren lands;

To be looked upon as peons, unworthy for a better life,
Subjected by the American government,
Who won't call these atrocities genocide;

How can we not speak of the forgotten ones,
Whose blood has soaked our lands,
And look each other in the eyes,
Like genocide has never even happened on our lands.
Who nowadays speaks of the forgotten ones,

Of the Afro-American (Black slaves) race,
Whose lives have been ravaged
By the genocidal hands of their oppressors;

Who nowadays speaks of the millions of Africans
Who had been kidnapped by the other African tribes,
And sold to slavery to Europeans to be transported by ship
Across the North Atlantic Ocean from the West Africa
To the America's Atlantic coast,
And resold back into slavery;

And of Africans who never made it across the ocean,
As their live bodies were thrown overboard;

And how the chattel, slavery system been rooted
Into the African race, and viewed by their oppressors,
The white-European-Americans, as three-fifth a man,
Like they were animals, savages, not human;

To be incarcerated by their slave-masters
On the plantations where they were beaten, raped,
Tortured, murdered, bred like farm animals,
As children were torn from their mothers' bosoms
And sold or exchanged for a financial gain;

And how they worked their fingers to the bone
By picking cotton under the scorching sun
That burned the skin off the slaves whipped backs;

To be colonized, exploited, controlled to such degree
That their whole way of life had been eliminated,
As their cultures, languages, traditions, religions
Eradicated out of their ethnicity forever
During those one hundred fifty years of bloody slavery;

How can we not speak of the forgotten ones,
Whose blood has soaked our lands,
And look each other in the eyes,
And talk of peace, human rights, mass incarceration,
Justice for all, and still won't call
These atrocities as genocide.

Who nowadays speaks of the forgotten ones,
Of the Jewish-Europeans,
Whose lives have been ravaged
By the genocidal hands of their oppressors;

Who nowadays speaks of the six and a half million Jews
Who had been annihilated during WWII,
By the Europeans and the Nazi[19] Germans,
From the European lands;

Evicted from their homes, treated like criminals,
Cancer of the nation, and sent on mass deportations
On the Train Wagons packed to its full capacity
Without room to breathe, without food, water
And access to basic human needs for many days,
To the concentration camps;

To be humiliated, beaten, tortured, murdered
And forced to commit despicable acts
Against their own people by the Nazis and their allies,
Who took part in carrying out sadistic acts
Against all humanity in the concentration camps;

Sent to the gas chambers,[20]

---

19      A German fascist party, from 1933 – 1945.
20      An airtight room that is filled with poisonous gas to kill prison-

And burned to ashes like pieces of wood;
Have Jewish children torn from their mothers, fathers,
Grandparents, never to be seen as a whole family again;

To constantly think of how to survive
Another day, another minute, another second;

To have hope to see a loved one again,
To lose hope and find hope
In the midst of the lost hope;

How can we not speak of the forgotten ones,
Whose blood has soaked our lands,
And look each other in the eyes,
And say Never Again!
And then again stand and watch
The slaughter of another nation to go on
And call it everything else, but genocide;

Who nowadays speaks of the forgotten ones,
Of the Cambodian (Khmer) people,
Whose lives have been ravaged
By the genocidal hands of their oppressors;

Who nowadays speaks of the one and two and a half
Millions of Cambodians who had been wiped out
Through either massacre or work to death
In forced labor camps during the bloody years
Of 1975 to 1979, by the Communist forces
Of the Khmer Rouge,[21] from the Southeast Asian land;
And how hundreds of thousands of Khmer people

---

ers.

21      (Red Khmer) a Cambodian Communist movement that was
active as a Guerilla force from 1970 to the late 1990s.

Were forced to flee their land,
And become refugees in the unknown lands;

As the Cambodian – Communist forces of the Khmer Rouge,
Under the leadership of Pol Pot,[22]
Launched a reign of Holocaust upon their own people;

And how millions of farmers, teachers, civil servants,
Army officers, countless ethnic Chinese and Vietnamese,
Who lived on the Southeast Asian land,
Particularly intellectuals who posed a threat
To the Communist regime, for they kept people enlightened
With the truth about their oppressors,
Were all arrested, tortured, and put to death;

And how the entire Khmer society were forced
To convert to Marxist ideology,
As Communists nationalized private properties,
Abolished money, suppressed religious practices
That has been part of the Khmer people
For over a thousand years;

Enforced communal living,
And controlled the entire country to such a degree
That it became a plantation,
The society became the slaves,
And the Communists their slave-masters;

How can we not speak of the forgotten ones,
Whose blood has soaked our lands,
And look each other in the eyes,
And call ourselves an intelligent race,
And yet again repeat the same mistakes

22      Cambodian political leader of the Khmer Rouge.

As we commit atrocities against our own race;

Who nowadays speaks of the forgotten ones,
Of the Rwandan (Tutsi) people,
Whose lives have been ravaged
By the genocidal hands of their oppressors;

Who nowadays speaks of the eight-hundred thousand Tutsis
Who had been annihilated, butchered by machetes
In one hundred days during 1994,
By their next door neighbors, Hutus,
From the Central African land;

And how the spread of hateful and inciteful words
By the Rwandan government's propaganda
Instilled the fear in Hutus eyes,
By reminding them of 1988;

Where Tutsi army killed one-hundred thousands Hutus
In cold blood, in retaliation of Hutus killing
One thousand Tutsis during the riots;

And how Hutus held on to their revenge
To avenge one-hundred thousands fallen Hutus,
And labeled any Hutu as enemy of the state,
If he or she would not take part
In killing their Tutsi neighbors;

And as ethnic violence erupted,
Tutsis' innocent blood spilled on the Central African land,
While the whole world stood and watched,
And did not call it for what it was,
Until it came to an end;

How can we not speak of the forgotten ones,
Whose blood has soaked our lands,
And look each other in the eyes,
And call ourselves children of God,
And say, "love your neighbor as yourself,"
But then seek revenge in the most atrocious way;

For those who stand and watch
As genocide unleased upon another race,
Are just as much to blame
Of these atrocious crimes;

For when we turn our backs
On innocent whose blood is spilled,
The vicious cycle of the genocide
Repeats itself again.

January 26, 2020

# Sorrow of the Ocean

By Artem Vaskanyan

I am always scared
To see you dive
Into my sorrow of the ocean
And not come out of it alive;

For any person who reaches
The bottom of my ocean
Will surely lose its mind,
Will surely drown
In the sorrow of my ocean;

Unless, your sorrow of the ocean
Is just as painful
As it is mine.

February 4, 2020

# A FAVOR
By Artem Vaskanyan

Gravedigger, Gravedigger, do me a favor,
Find me a resting place
Where no man had ever
Set foot on this place.

Gravedigger, Gravedigger, dig me a grave,
On top of the mountain
Closer to stars;

In a place where no airy souls
Could ever reach its peak,
Nor for any man to ever bring
Its sorrow and pain.

Gravedigger, Gravedigger, dig me a grave,
So you could lay my body to rest
In unnamed grave;

No tombstone is needed over my grave,
Just lay enough cobblestones to mark my grave
In the form of the ring,
To represent perpetual cycle of pain and suffering
That I had endured,
Here on this fertile loam of dirt.

Gravedigger, Gravedigger, Oh, don't you dare,
To bury me next to
Some unknown soul,
And for all eternity;

For if you can't find me

My resting place
That I so desperately crave,
Then don't even bother
To lay me to rest;

For I know that my spirit will not rest
From seeing my body lying next to
Some poor soul,
Whose people will come to its grave
And grieve over its lost soul,
And in the process disturb my grave
With their sorrow and pain;

For if I can't rest in one peace
Away from a scene of uproar and confusion,
Under the stars caressing my grave,
And the moon illuminating my resting place,
Then I would rather be cremated instead;

And have my ashes scattered
From the highest peak
Into the high winds,
To carry me across the ancient lands
Where once my ancestors
Had roamed these lands;

So one day, I could return
To my resting place
From where I was risen
In the first place.

Oh, Gravedigger, Gravedigger, believe it or not,
But for half of my life
I have always had

Mastery over my crestfallen life;

So for me to ask for this favor
Is quite a lot;

And it's not the pride nor my ego,
That my spirit won't allow me
To be laid next to
Some unknown soul;

But from being awake
For half of my life,
From the same ignorance
That I was drunk upon once;

Which didn't allow me to see
How all mankind sell their precious soul,
In exchange to escape a bitter life,
Just to have a taste
Of a short sweet life,
In the bitter world.

February 11, 2020

# FATHER! HAVE MERCY,
By Artem Vaskanyan

Father! Have mercy, on our souls,
For we do not know what we do and say.

Father! Have mercy, on all ignorant beings
Who do not believe that all mortal souls can change,
And yet, they seek forgiveness for themselves,
And insist to be recognized
That they have changed,
As they continue to judge, stigmatize,
And condemn without trial all mankind,
And say that they cannot be changed.

Father! Have mercy, on all hypocrite beings,
For they are not different from those
Who punish people with their poisonous words;

Who go to a place of worship and preach God's words,
And yet, cannot apply what they teach
To their own self-righteous lives.

Father! Have mercy, on all narrow-minded beings,
Clear their clouded minds,
Pull the specks out of their eyes,
And help them see and understand
That no man is made perfect, nor omnipotent;

And that the only difference
Between these mortal souls and those,
Is their daily actions
That define for who they are.

Father! Have mercy, on our souls,
For we do not know what we do and say;

For if we knew and truly understood our wicked acts,
Then we would have never dared
To look each other in the eyes,
And act in such a wicked way
Without feeling ashamed from what we do and say.

February 13, 202

# DANDELION
By Artem Vaskanyan

It was not the ambrosiatic aroma
From the Lilac flowers
That spun my head,

Nor divine omnipresence
From the forest in leaf
That caused my heart
To bloom with bliss,

Nor mellifluous chant
From the close by creek
That made my soul
Dance and sing,

But the promising feeling in my sixth –
Followed by the appearance
Of pure beauty
That I caught
From the corner of my eye,
That made me turn my head
One hundred and eight-two degrees,
And see –
How she stood still before me
Like a Dandelion,
Unwafted by the breeze
In the middle of the lea.

February 18, 2020

# REJECTION
By Artem Vaskanyan

Rejection is a path
To a sublime life.

Without rejection,
There can be –
No perfection,
No self-realization,
No awe-inspiring –
Change in life.

Rejection, after rejection –
Brings an ominous feeling
Of disgust,
Like being damned,
Forsaken by god –
Knows who or what.

Rejection is painful!

Rejection tears a soul apart,
But in the process
It opens up the mind,
To look, and see the life
Through a different set of eyes,
And create an awe-inspiring beauty
Out-of-life.

February 21, 2020

# Au revoir!
By Artem Vaskanyan

It is a privilege to know
The time of one's death;

For death strikes
When least expected
Without a time to say,
Au revoir!

Death came for my father,
In a form of Cancer,
Quite unexpectedly;

Almost robbed me of my brother,
Quite surprisingly;

And, it even came
For some of my dear friends,
Quite successfully;

It showed them, No Mercy!
Until the very end;

As it drained their lives, slowly,
Like a parasite,
Quite malevolently;

It did not discriminate against
Age-race-gender,
Nor who's good or bad;

It came for the all,

All the same,
Out-of-nowhere
Like a wind
Steals a breath;

But, at least it gave them
Little time, to Stop!

Ruminate on Life!

And, appreciate every moment,
Every breath —

And, before the end, say,
Au revoir!

To all the loved ones
Whom they hold dear in their hearts
As they leave them all behind.

February 26, 2020

# SILENCE!
By Artem Vaskanyan

It was one of those nights,
They call it a white night.
Where I laid in bed
Exhausted from the hard days' work,
Craving to sleep, and yet!
I was wide awake
From the loud noise.

I put my ear plugs in
To minimize some of the senseless shouting,
But that didn't work.

I turned on the only fan I had
To full blast,
To drown some of the raucous with white noise,
And still I heard the senseless shouting,
And the music raving,
Creeping through beneath the cracks
Of front door.

I paused, and thought,
Am I the only one
Who hasn't lost his mind?

To think that it's crazy
To act like a belligerent nincompoop,
In the middle of the night.

I must confess what's on my mind,
For it's eating me alive.
That I'm appalled to see

Grown – men – and – women,
Act like children,
Who laugh and joke and scream
Like fools, All Day Long.

They have grown physically!
But, intellectually?
Their minds have never evolved,
Never matured to meet their age,
As a result, it left their spirits
In a dormant state.

I know!
It's what most of the people crave,
To scream, and yell, and party all night.
But there must be some kind of order,
Some kind of rules that state:

For how long!  How loud!  When!  Where!
They get to scream and yell
Like Lunatics, All Day Long.

I tried to read,
That didn't work.
It only upset me even more.

And so! I began to write, and tell
Exactly how I felt
When loud mouths right next door
Won't let me sleep
In the middle of the night.

The ear-splitting screams of men and women
Sounded like senseless cries

Of macaques at the zoo.

What can I say? What can I do?
I live right next to them next door.
Whether I like it, or not,
They're my neighbors after all
Who just won't work with me,
Or try to understand

That I've got to get up at dawn
And work till dusk,
In the place that is just as loud
As my home.

Should I come out once again?
Knock and say,
"Shut the Fuck Up!!!'
But that won't fix the problem,
It will only make it worse,
Like it did last time.

Nowadays, I try to love my neighbor as myself,
But that is more easily said than done.

I paused, and took a deep breath in, again.
And slowly exhaled, and pondered my thoughts,
And scribbled in my pad,
Exactly what I thought;

'Ignorance, can't be met with ignorance,
It just won't work,
It will only start the war
Between two neighbors,
Like it always does.'

There has to be another way,
To reach out to these folks,
And find the same language that they speak,
In hopes of understanding one another
In a better way.

But wait!
I've tried that already last week.
Talking to my neighbors,
Is like talking to a wall
That echoes back at me,
My exact words;

I said, exactly as I recall,
And as politely as I could,
Holding my temper back,
As they opened the door
After a loud knock.

'Silence!
I call upon those
Who give in so easily to noise,
Just to hear themselves talk
As they spit out meaningless words;

'Whose words are nothing more
Than just a frivolous noise
That comes out of fear
To welcome silence into their hearts;

'For silence, is a peace of mind,
Unwillingly forces one to ruminate on life,
And reveal to yourself,
The person that you are,

The person that you could become —

'If only silence was embraced
For just a breath . . .
Then you would see
That your words are just a noise,
A waste of time,
A waste of precious breath,
That have no power to move people's hearts
Nor touch their souls.'

The look they gave me, was,
Go To Hell!

But I didn't judge,
Nor even get upset,
For I used to be just like them
With the same crazy look in their eyes,
Who never listened, or took advice
From any elderly who preached,
Or any one with more brains than I.

And so, I endured their judgmental eyes
As I walked away;
But I at least, sowed a seed;

A seed of silence in their hearts
That I know for sure,
One day will sprout
And transform their hearts
From noise to silence.

March 5, 2020

# LA VARICELLA
By Artem Vaskanyan

At first, I thought it was the garlic
That made me sick,
But it was not!
And I didn't realize that at the beginning.

Not until, I ended up in isolation,
But only this time it was not
Because of my mischievous behavior,
But instead, of some viral infection
That I contracted from who knows who or what.

It caused my body to cover with bumps and blisters
That even Doctors were not sure, at first,
What I had;
Even though they did suspect that it was,
La Varicella!

"La Varicella," as the Hispanic Doctor called it,
And then translated into English
For what it meant, "The Chicken Pox."

In my forty years, I've never had,
Such a severe viral infection as this;
Could someone have coughed or sneezed
Around me since Thursday?

For it was late at night
That I started to feel the chills and slightly
Break out mostly around my face;

And since I felt the sickness right after I ate

A few cloves of garlic with a "Ramen" soup,
I thought it was the garlic
That made me sick,
And I swore to never eat it again.

But who could it be,
That gave me this nasty viral infection then?
I keep going over and over in my head,
Replaying every little encounter that I had
With a sick person that ill-fated day.

I was furious with the person who made me sick,
And wanted some kind of revenge in exchange –
But, it's impossible to tell
Who the carrier was;

Since everyone who lives and works around me
Is sick like a dog!

For five alarming days,
I was quarantined in an empty cell by the doctors
Out of fear that I could spread La Varicella.

But I didn't mind, for I was in an awful shape,
And didn't want to be seen or disturbed by anyone;
Besides, I didn't want to be the carrier of La Varicella,
Be that same guy who I'm furious with.

And to be frank,
I was grateful for what I had,
Since it could've been much worse than that.

It's not only La Varicella,
Or the seasonal flu

That is going around nowadays,
But much worse that the world has seen.

They call it the Covid-19, the Coronavirus,
Or as Trump prefers to call it,
"The Chinese Virus."

March 7, 2020

# Too Late
By Artem Vaskanyan

When we were close,
I only seemed to remember
Bad things about you;

But when we became apart,
I started to remember
Only good about you;

But by then,
It was too late,

For you were gone, long gone,
And were never coming back
Into my life again.

April 1, 2020

# Los Lobos Domesticados[23]
By Artem Vaskanyan

Los lobos domesticados
Never bite, but always bark;
They speak de amor[24] and preach de Dios,[25]
But hate with pasión[26] any one
Who keeps ones espíritu[27] impeccably intact.
They walk and talk with heads held high
And keep el hombre,[28]
The keeper de hombres,[29]
The same man who puts the leash on them, Contento,[30]
As much as they posiblemente[31] can;
They are adicto[32] to their leash,
And never leave without it,
For they believe en verdad[33]
That they were born with it;
Las almas![34] de los lobos domesticados
Have been ripped right out of them
From the first momento[35]
When they stopped luchando,[36]

---

23    The Domesticated Wolves.
24    Of love.
25    Of God.
26    Passion.
27    Spirit.
28    The man.
29    Of men.
30    Content/Happy.
31    Possibly.
32    Addicted.
33    Truly.
34    The Souls!
35    Moment.
36    Fighting.

For their libertad.[37]

April 9, 2020

---

37     Freedom.

# HERMITLIKE
By Artem Vaskanyan

Alone, like a hermit,
Without a single soul
Whom I can call,
And share my thoughts with
And yet, at the same time
I feel just fine
Like I have all the love
And support I need
To have a fruitful life.

For I have myself, the self,
That has cultivated all the necessary tools
To help me deal with isolation.

I have my Yoga practice,
The prajna parmita,[38]
And unshakable belief in my Creator,
To keep me grounded, strong,
And all around, sacred.

It is the sole reason why,
I feel stronger than most of the men
During the time of total isolation,

For I rely on nothing else,
But my practice and belief,
To help me overcome
Whatever may come my way.

Men who rely on comfort, love and support

38      Perfection of wisdom.

From family and friends,
Instead of adamantly strengthening
Their practice and belief,
And searching for the missing piece
To fill the hole within their heart,
In time will feel abandoned and alone
When they end up in isolation.

Since, once the temporary comfort,
Love and support is gone,
They will begin to lose themselves,
To their own self, piece by piece,
Like a page by page is being ripped
Out of a book, Until,
Not a single leaf is left inside,
But, just a cover of the empty book.

I know this from personal experience
That I myself have painfully endured,
That comfort, love and support
Just doesn't last too long;

For when I depended on another to survive,
I gave the power to another over my life,
And I began to feel like I was a pawn,
In a game of chess.

It was only during the time
Of total isolation,
And complete surrender of myself,
That I could tell
How strong my practice was.

The greatest life achievements

That I accomplished were
In the darkest, most isolated places
From where I only saw
The top of the trees,
And dreamed about seeing
The bottom of those trees one day.

April 13, 2020

# SURVIVING ISN'T LIVING
By Artem Vaskanyan

Surviving isn't living.
Since, from the first moment
When you start caring
Only about yourself,
You stop living,
And start surviving instead;

For living has to do with
Caring for others
While surviving is only
Caring about yourself.

Thus, a man, who is surviving
Cannot conceivably enjoy
The fruits of life
To its fullest.

April 19, 2020

# Never Settle
By Artem Vaskanyan

Entered into a place
Of hate and misery
From a place of love and joy
Where I've seen and lived
A life of pleasure,
And this is why!
I'll always fight
For a life of higher caliber,
And never settle for a lesser price.

April 20, 2020

# ALL I EVER WANTED . . .

### By Artem Vaskanyan

All I ever wanted was,
Is to have my own little farm,

Plant trees and watch them grow
From my cabin's porch,

Wake up to the melodious sound of
Cock-a-doodle-doo!

Watch the sunrise, rise!
Over the trees and mountains,
As I produce my magnum opus;[39]

And spend the rest of my life
Searching for something mysterious,
And in the process of finding it,
Becoming strong enough
To let it go.

All I ever wanted was,
A second chance.

April 22, 2020

---

39 The greatest work of art, music or literature that a person has created.

# THE LOCKDOWN
By Artem Vaskanyan

Alone, I sit on the bed,
Behind closed barred doors
And ruminate on my thoughts . . .

My cell, is the death cell!
For the nurses and the guards
Can easily leave me here to die.

My survival depends on them,
For it's they who bring me food and medicine,
And along with it the Coronavirus.

It's been weeks,
Since they locked the prison down,
Out of fear that the Covid-19
Might spread inside the prison walls.

It feels like prison within the prison
And the walls are closing in on me.

For every country in the world
Is on a lock down as well.

The fear of contracting the Coronavirus
Grows stronger amongst men each day.

Everyone thinks for oneself,
No one feels safe,
And, no one trusts each other,
Not that any of them did before,
But they most definitely do act

More paranoid than ever before.

And they are right to do so,
For the virus doesn't discriminate against anyone.

This virus had already taken
More lives around the world
Than anyone had ever predicted.

And it appears that it's only the beginning,
Which will last for a few years more;

Since, the virus has put
The whole world on a lockdown,
Crippled the economy globally within weeks,
And continues to kill by the thousands
Around the world every day.

It's Terrifying!
Even from where I am,
For it feels like some science fiction story,
Where the entire world
Is coming to an end.

Never in my life time
Did I expect it to happen for real,
It seems biblical and surreal.

Yet, it's happening,
As it unravels right in front of my eyes.

I'm certain that . . .
"The free people" around the world,
The ones who are outside the prison walls,

Who sit at home during the lockdown
And not being able to go out
To work, and mingle with family and friends,
Will start to understand
What prison life is like,
And how it feels to be isolated
From life itself.

And yet, when millions around the world
Are imprisoned,
Endure the pain of isolation
Every day,
Only a handful of people
Protest and speak of them,
While the rest stay silent,
Until it happens to them.

I guess . . .
Seeing people being isolated
And treated like animals
Was never a grave issue for you,
Until it started to happen to you!

How hypocritical of you!

It's the same as to speak of evil
That had been done to you,
But never speak of evil
That had been done by you.

April 26, 2020

# An Empty House
By Artem Vaskanyan

I lived in an empty house
Built out of matches
That one day lit up
Like a Christmas tree
And burned to the ground,
Leaving me stranded and alone,
And exhausted to my bones.

Ever since that tragic day
I haven't been the same,
For when I lost my place,
I also lost my way.

I've been trying to rebuild
From the ground up
What I had lost,
But, the only problem always was,
That I only had the matches
To build my house with.

I moved from place to place,
But, somehow in the end,
It always was
Just like my other place

The same empty house
That every time when I come in,
It turns into a living Hell for me.

I blamed the place for being grotesque,
But not myself

Who lived in it.

I guess, I just couldn't
Admit the truth to myself,
That the problem lied within me
And not with the place.

It dawned on me,
Like the first appearance of light
In the morning,
Shines through the window
On my dormant eyes.

What I bring with me
Into an empty house
Is what I'll fill it with,
And that's what
Will become of it for me.

An empty house is just like
Any other empty place
That craves for a living soul
To occupy its empty space,
And bring it into life.

For it's I,
And not the place
That turns it into Hell
Or Nirvana.

If you can't change the place
That you find yourself living in
Then change yourself,
Before it lights up

Like a Christmas tree,
And burns to the ground
Just like it did with me.

April 29, 2020

# THE AUGUST TREE
By Artem Vaskanyan

There is a majestic-ebonic-dense tree
That stands for eons
By the creek,

Whose roots extend for miles
Deep down into the dirt
And suck insatiably on water
From the well's creek.

It's denser with foliage in August
Than any tree in its vicinity.

And just like every leaf
On the branches of its tree
Is different from another,

So is every life form
That dwells around it
From each other.

It speaks!
With a gentle voice
Of a whooshing sound
From the rustling leaves,
When the gentle breeze
Picks up and sways its branches;

It listens!
With a silent stillness,

When nightfall comes

And yellow-reddish moon appears
With countless sparkling-orbiting stars
Above its august crown;

It bears!
A legion of mouthwatering fruits
With a hidden seed of life,
In each —

As an eternal gift,
For being brought back to bear life
On August of each year.

As it drops suddenly many fruits
Like cloudburst bursts into tears
From high above
To feed all life.

Some say!
The first seed of the august tree
Fell from the sky
With the morning star, in August,

On the same spot
Where now it stands.

But others say!
The first seed of the august tree
Was planted eons ago
By the hand of the Creator.

For all life to feed upon
And plant its seeds
For future life,

Just like once
It was done for us.

May 5, 2020

# THE ENERGY OF LOVE
### By Artem Vaskanyan

Today I felt the energy of love
Running through my veins,
First time in twenty gloomy years
When I spoke with a young lady on a phone
Who made me feel alive
With her gentle voice.

Today has passed into another day
And still I feel the energy of love
Running through my veins,
As it gives me hope
To live better than those gloomy days,
In now these brighter days.

Today again has passed
Into another day,
And I'm grateful even more
Than I was a day before
For the pleasant moment such as this.

For I feel even more in love today
From being alive,
As the energy of love
Keeps running through my veins;

And in the process recuperates
What has been lost,
But not forgotten
Within my fractured soul,
To what it once long time ago was,
Since I could last recall.

Today again has passed
Into another – another day,
Since last time I heard her gentle voice
And mellifluous sounds of her laughter.

Yet still, till this very day,
Her soothing voice
And sweet-sounding laughter
Continues to echo in my soul
And bring my intoxicated heart
In the middle of the night
To laughter.

Although, I've never seen her
Nor felt her presence by my side,
I feel as I, have known her
All those gloomy years of my life.

Perhaps it's true!
What some rarely say
About those who were destined
To fall apart and perish;

That a man who has been cast away
And long forgotten,
Can feel the energy of love
In such an exotic way
That many never will,
Until they too find themselves cast away
And long forgotten.

2020

# WITHOUT YOU

By Artem Vaskanyan

It wasn't the color or your eyes,
Or the color of your hair,
Nor the way you moved your body,
When you danced and sang;

Bu the way you smiled
When you saw me standing
In the middle of the road
Watching you.

That's what makes me think of you
Every single moment
When I'm losing you;

And if one day,
You would fade away
Leaving me broken-hearted and alone,

I, would then, Not accept this
As the end to us.

I would roam to the ends of the world
Relentlessly, in search of you;
And if I were to discover
No existing presence of you,

I, would then, happily drink
The Hemlock,
And ascend into the high and low
Realms, in search of you,
- for all the lifespans

That my soul could bare;

And if the God will chose
To take my soul,
And give your soul to the Devil,

I, would then, find a way
To escape from the Heavens
And enter into the realms of Hell;

So I could spend my whole eternity
Being next to you;

Since when you're with me,
Hell is Heaven in every way to me
While Heaven is a living Hell without you.

October, 2020

# THE CREATOR
By Artem Vaskanyan

You're in every
Light
dark or bright
Flower
withered or alive
Breath
first to last
Life
birth to death
Soul
virtuous to wicked
Work of art     Beating heart     Errant mind
Smile
tear shed
Grain of sand
Fallen raindrop
send

October 19, 2020

# AZURE

By Artem Vaskanyan

I thought of you
As I laid on a lea,
Listening to the sweet melancholic melody
Of a violin,

And the more I thought of you,
The more my sorrow grew,
Tearing my heart inside out
From not being next to you,

And it's not the distance
That keeps us apart,
But my ill-fated circumstance
That will not allow
For our paths to cross,

I look into the azure sky,
And pluck a cloud with my eyes
That has your features,

I feel your presence suddenly arise,
Like you are lying next to me
With an azaleas woven
Into your bright blue colored hair,

And without a single uttered word,
With a deep piercing gaze
Into your azure eyes,
I say,
a thousand sweet-kind words,

October 20, 2020

# The Same Mistake
By Artem Vaskanyan

At times,
I would rather trust the Devil
Than a human being!

For at least I know for sure
What kind of a soul dwells within
The Devil's spirit.

But within a human being!
Its spirit has most definitely
More than one soul,
The good, the wicked and
Something else that lurks in between
That till this day
I still haven't figured out.

These human beings always use
The same technique on me.

First the good, to disarm my barriers,
And then, once I become vulnerable
They throw their wickedness at me.

I keep making the same mistake
When it comes down to dealing with
Human beings;

Trusting them way too soon,
Instead of first taking my sweet time with them
To see the true nature of their souls;

And, it is always the good part of my soul
That keeps letting me drop my guard down
And stay alert.

When it reminds me of compassion, forgiveness,
And to forget my last encounter that I had
With the wicked soul
That nearly cost me to dwell
My entire life in Hell.

January 11, 2021

# My Garden

By Artem Vaskanyan

My garden is surrounded by the suffocating walls,
The same walls that try to tame me
Like a savage beast inside the cage;
But all the flowers in my garden
Can only feel the presence of the sun
And stars beyond the sky,
And when I pour rain water over them.

When my heart feels gloom by the suffocating walls,
I, then go and visit the flowers in my garden
Who remind me of a beautiful life
That exists beyond these walls.

I guard my garden and I nurture my flowers
More than my own heart,
For I grow them not for me
But for someone who is very dear to me.

My garden is truly alive!
For when I sow with love
My flowers bloom in color        Bright-red;

But when I sow with loathe,
Then they bloom                Dark-red,
And I reap exactly what I sow in the end.

The flowers in my garden know me well!
For when my heart becomes fermented
By the poison of the suffocating walls,
Then all the flowers in my garden
Begin to wither and die off

Like they have been grown in a desert
Without a drop of rain and love.

January 24, 2021

# A Bird
### By Artem Vaskanyan

Democracy is like a bird
Hovering over its free land,

And every time when an abuse of power transpires
On its land,
It plucks the feathers from the bird's wings,

Until they are so weaken that they give in
And the bird plummets onto its land.

Where from now on it will remain to crawl
With wings that can no longer fly
On no longer called free land,

Where the heart of the Democracy has been destroyed
By abuse of power.

February 5, 2021

# BOUND

By Artem Vaskanyan

I am bound to your words
Of being no more than your friend
And I dare not to cross the line
For I am scared to lose you as my friend.

But if you would one day decide to break the rule,
As for us being more than just close friends,
I, then with every fiber of my body will acquiesce,
And say to you, Yes!

For I believe with all my heart
That every friendship must continue to evolve,
Since when it ceases to progress,
Then it becomes as stagnant as the water in the pond
And then turns into a swamp.

And so, in the name of our friendship, sort of speak,
We both must try to flow together as one creek
To go through any barriers like a river –
Cuts through the rocks,

Until we flow into the Ocean
Where we could freely expand our minds
Without being bound to any words.

- 2021

# The Test
### By Artem Vaskanyan

The true essence of my soul was put to a test the other day,
When an agent from the F.B.I. came to see me,
And offered to release me, but only for a price.

He was such a pleasant, kind gentleman
That I felt guilty when I said, No! to him,
Since the price for my freedom was too high
For my soul to bare.

It is not in my nature nor in the heart of my soul
To go down that soul-crushing path,
Where I would have to turn into a treacherous man
And set traps for another,
Who could end up like an animal in a cage.

As much as I want with every fiber of my body
To be free from all
That I've endured for over twenty years;

The heart of my soul just won't allow me
To take such a soul-wrecking path in life,
Easing my pain and suffering
At the expense of bringing miser and destruction
Upon another unenlightened man.

The preservation of my soul is more valuable to me
Than a free life. It is priceless in every way.

And to help to destroy an unenlightened man
At the expense of exposing my soul by becoming wicked,
Is not the true way for any man to live his life

Who values the heart of his soul.

I have no ego left in me,
But whatever was in me was proud of myself;
For I had passed the test once again,
Since it was not the first time
When a sweet deal was offered to me by similar gentle-man.

The first time I refused was purely out of pride,
And the code that I live by to this day;
But this time it was for a much higher moral principle.

I know that many men like I,
Who are serving draconian sentences in prison
Would not miss such opportunity in life,
But that is because the hearts of their souls are treacherous,
They are rotten to the core.

Men like that are dangerous.
For if they have No honor!
No self-respect!
No true way in life!

Then these men are capable of crossing the line,
That thin line that stands between a man and an animal,
From committing crimes so despicable
That it becomes impossible to believe
That there is a living soul
That dwells within their hearts.

To me, it absolutely matters how I live,
And survive in this earthly realm.

Since I believe with every fiber in my body

That the way a man lives his life in this realm,
Is exactly how he will dwell in the next.

February 12, 2021

# THE KEEPER OF MEN
By Artem Vaskanyan

I often wonder!
How can a man keep another shackled, hand cuffed
And locked away inside a cage to suffer
For all eternity, but then,
Treat a stray dog better than a man he keeps . . .

It is difficult, almost impossible not to feel
Any loathe for a Keeper of men;
For what he does to another man
Is truly the worst of all beasts.

He is a servant of the Devil in the earthly realm,
A tormentor of the human souls he keeps . . .

To make a living of another man's pain and suffering
Is one of the most disgusting acts
That any man can find a way to live his life.

Not only is it a crime against mankind,
But it is the most detrimental act
That the Keeper of men can afflict upon one's own soul.

Perhaps if one, would've experienced the same shackled life
By the hand of the Keeper of men,
Then he would've too developed such loathe for him or her.

I say it, because I seen it with my own eyes.
I felt it on my own skin,
And heard the cries of many tormented men
Amongst whose cry was often mine.

I was in distraught from internal pain
By being treated like I was not even a man.
It made me feel like my body was not even mine
Like it didn't even belong to me,
Only my mind was left to me
And its ruminating thoughts that flowed through it.

The prayers did not always help
And there was no one else to ask for help.

I only found comfort in my tears,
When the Keeper of men was not in sight
To keep his eyes on all the beasts like I,
Who was grappling within themselves
To fall asleep at night.

I cursed the God so many times at night
That I started to believe that I was cursed by him
Since the first moment I saw light.

When hope died within my heart,
I wished to start the process of life again;
Since death was much easier to embrace
Than my shackled life,
Which had only one meaning to me at that time,
To suffer, suffer to the end.

At times the only way for me
Was to escape from all of this
Was to ruminate relentlessly,
Imagining myself to have wings like raven,
And take flight into the heart of the sky
Where no one could ever cause any pain and suffering to me.

No one ever came knocking on my door to offer help.
The Keeper of men has always made sure of that
As he or she stood in the way
Like a Demon with a giant axe,
Preventing any benevolent – free man
To ever come and offer help.

February 15, 2021

# All We Left With
By Artem Vaskanyan

We all know that life can end at any moment,
Even though we often ignore this fact;

But when someone close to us encounters death
Then we begin to acknowledge
That death is closer than we thought it was.

None of our possessions,
Nor our loved ones
Can come with us;

And our bodies no matter how strong
And beautiful they are,
No longer good to us.

All we left with is,
What we had gathered in our souls
From being on the spiritual path
Throughout our lives.

March 15, 2021

# A RESERVOIR
By Artem Vaskanyan

There is a reservoir as big as the Ocean
That lives inside of every man.

Yet, you search like a blind man
Outside yourself to satisfy your thirst.
While everything that you have ever needed
To live richer than any happy Ruler
Already exists inside of you.

You are a reservoir as big as the Ocean,
Yet, you live like a desert
That has not seen a drop of rain in eons;

And roam the lands like a vagabond
In hopes to satisfy your inner thirst,
As you beg for a sip of water
From a dried up well.

March 19, 2021

# LOVE AND POETRY
### By Artem Vaskanyan

Love and poetry are so much alike
Since they both require a great deal of honesty,
And being true to oneself
Is the most essential part
Of being an ardent flower
And a creative artist of great sensitivity.

Love is just like poetry,
Where it is impossible for an ardent flower
To win over one's heart
Without first revealing the heart of one's soul
To the one an ardent flower is unconditionally in love;

And so is the same with poetry.
Where it is impossible for a creative artist of great sensitivity
To create an art of work
Without first revealing the heart of one's soul
To one's poem.

March 20, 2021

# PRICELESS
By Artem Vaskanyan

A man without freedom is a slave
And there is just no other way to put it.

They say that slavery had been abolished
On February 1st, 1865,
And yet, we still crawl desperately on our knees
Inside our little caves like blind people,
And beg to be let out.

They say, if freedom was easily attained
Then there would be nothing special about it,
And so they continue to keep us in our caves
Just to make their point.

You can only understand how priceless freedom is,
When you had held it in your hands
And then lost it.

And only after you had dug
With your bare hands,
To crawl out of the cave
That was as black as blindness,

Do you start to appreciate the light
And realize that what you lost
Was truly priceless.

Close your eyes inside your little cave
And feel the darkness engulfing you.
The despair and loneliness entering your heart
And the chains binding you.

Now! Open your eyes
And feel the light shining upon you,
The joy entering your heart,
And the chains unbinding you;

And that is as close as I can get
To my priceless.

March, 2021

# Two Forces

By Artem Vaskanyan

Just as there are no souls
That are exactly alike
Only that they share the same path in life;

So is the same with all the spirits
Whose purpose is to give life
To the souls that inhabit menkind.

In a man two energies exist,
The soul and the spirit.

The soul is the moral force,
While the spirit is the life giving force.
Both mysteriously appear in a man
Out of the blue,
Where they begin to dwell.

And although, they are completely
Of two different energies,
Yet, they cannot exist in a man
One without another.

The spirit passes from being to being
Like river flows through the rocks,
While the soul is like a star in the cosmos
Appears out of the blue to shine,
Until it falls into an unknown;

And just like there are no eyes
That are exactly alike,
Only that they share the same purpose in life;

So is the same with all the souls and spirits
Whose purpose is to test
The force of their own will
In a man that they chose to possess
As it becomes their battle ground.

Just like some souls are wicked to the core
And some are virtuous,
So is the same with all the spirits
That dwell inside a man;

And this is why the soul and the spirit
Is always at war with each other to the end.

When the spirit and the soul are alike,
They merge,

And if they are both evil,
Then the evil prevails in a man over good
And this man becomes wicked,
And starts to interpret all good that he sees
Into his own image,
Perverting and twisting them
Into what lurks inside his dominated force,
The force that drives his moral principles.

And if they are both virtuous,
Then the good within him prevails over evil,
And this man becomes virtuous,
And starts to interpret all evil that he sees
Into his own image,
Changing and turning them
Into what lurks inside his dominating force,
The force that drives his moral principles.

But most men possess
The combination of them both,
And for that reason alone,
The war within a man
Never ceases to go on.

The wicked and the virtuous both see life
Thru their own set of eyes,
Framed by their own dominating force;

Neither of them are ideal,
Since they both possess ignorance and enlightenment
Which determines the way they see life,
Until the spirit and the soul
Will part from a man.

March 2021

# Samsara Realm
By Artem Vaskanyan

The earth is a Samsara Realm,
A place where a perpetual cycle
Of suffering never ends.

 It takes one year for the earthly realm
To go around the sun
And then the cycle of the suffering
Begins again.

It is a never ending journey in itself,
And everyone who dwells in the Samsara Realm
Are born, die, and reborn
Life after life,

Except for the ones who become Buddhas,
The Enlightened ones.

- 2021

# ON THE VERGE OF COLLAPSE
By Artem Vaskanyan

When you look around
And fail to see the beauty
In this world,
Then that is how you know
You are on the verge of collapse.

- 2021

# No Tears
### By Artem Vaskanyan

You can never understand
What's going through my mind
By simply looking at me from a great distance.

You must sit down with me one on one,
And have a heart to heart conversation
To truly grasp what lurks
Deep down in my heart
And why I shed no tears.

Just because you see no tears
In my eyes,
It doesn't mean that I'm not crying.

Everyone mourns in its own way
And the way I mourn
Is without tears.

It's only during my darkest days
Is when my soul is tested
And my spirit shows its strength the most.

When my time will come
To reveal the true essence of my soul
And the strength of my spirit,
Shed no tears for me
If I do fall;

But do remember me
The way I was
When I shed no tears.

March 31, 2021

# I Am

By Artem Vaskanyan

When people ask me
Of who I am,
I want to say to them,
I'm Soul-Spirit,
But I don't,

Instead I say to them,
The name that I was given,
And then, I don't say another word,
I let the silence take control;

Since, it is not easy to grasp
For just any man
That the name that is attached to all of us
And the place where we were born,
And the blood that flows through us,
And our ethnicity, culture, traditions,
And our religion that has been etched into us,
And all that we had mastered
Throughout our lives,
Is not what defines us,
It is not who we are.

When I say my name,
I often point to my chest
To reaffirm my statement;

But the truth is
That my body is just a flesh,
And my name is just a name
It is not who I am,

Or what defines me.

But what does!
Is the Soul-Spirit
That lives within me;

And the only time
When I feel internally connected
To my essence,
Is when I look in the mirror
And begin to stare
Into the depths of my eyes
And see the essence of my soul
Suddenly arise,

Looking back at me
With a glowing stare in my eyes,
As I feel the Spirit
Roaming throughout me;

And that is what truly defines me
And makes me who I am.

April 1, 2021

# CHANGE
By Artem Vaskanyan

You hardly have a power
To change yourself,
And yet, you go around
And try to change the other men,
Into what you often wished
You were yourself.

I never said that I was perfect,
But I did say
I like the way I am.

For I always look for a way
To improve myself
So I could become a better man.

And if you are taking me for granted
For the way I am,
Then let me be,
And go find yourself another man
Whom you can try to change
Into what you often wished
You were yourself.

Though, be careful what you wish for,
When you try to change other men,
For you might end up with someone
Who is just like yourself
Whom you've been trying to change
Into someone else
Ever since I've known you.

If change doesn't come
From within yourself,
Then it is impossible to transform yourself
Into someone you wish to become.

If change is what you seek,
Then first, change yourself;
For if you cannot change yourself
Then how do you expect to change
Other men.

April 2, 2021

# ACKNOWLEDGEMENTS

I am forever grateful to Boston University for offering a B.L.S. degree to the (MCI) Norfolk Prison, including all professors who never gave up coming to prison and teach despite all the harassments they had faced by the prison administration. Thank you for giving me an opportunity to get my education. Also, thank you to all Buddhist Theravada Monks and a Zen Monk, including all Buddhist volunteers who came to the Norfolk Prison's religious program for many years to teach Dharma (the Buddhist-Teachings). Thank you for helping me find my path in life and bringing me closer to enlightenment.

A Special Thank You! to my Bábushka (Grandmother) who was like my Mother, my sage, and my best friend, and to my Dédushka (Grandfather) who was like my Father; to my Brother Edgar and my Mom, thank you for your support; to my best friend, Maksim, for encouraging me to get my education; to my Partakers, Dave and Joyce, and Lise and Nelson, for coming to see me in prison, staying in touch, and not forgetting me; and to all my close friends for their constructive criticism, and support.

Thank you all for your friendship, love and support.